"Lucinda Secrest McDowell's beau  me deeper into the Word of God and clos

␣ebbie Macomber,
#1 ∧ .ork *Times* best-selling author

"Lucinda Secrest McDowell's books never disappoint—and this one is not to be missed! Every day we face important choices that alter our attitude, our outlook, our approach to people, and our spiritual productivity. *Life-Giving Choices* will greatly impact the way you live your life. She masterfully weaves powerful quotations with heart-gripping stories and applicable Scripture. Each day's topic concludes with a prayer and a question that will prompt you to take action. This timeless devotional is my go-to gift for friends and family members."

—Carol Kent,
speaker and author of *He Holds My Hand*

"As the champion of Encouraging Words, Lucinda Secrest McDowell's *Life-Giving Choices* devotional is a daily arrow pointing readers toward a more joyful, hopeful, and faithful life! Lucinda's easy writing style, tremendous godly wisdom, and sense of humor made this sixty-day devotional an opportunity that I looked forward to choosing to experience each day."

—Barb Roose,
speaker and author of *Winning the Worry Battle*

"We are able to choose what really matters because God provides endless resources to help us. We can choose authenticity, healing, obedience, serenity, and celebration—sixty choices that will lead to a more whole and holy life. Weaving humor, memorable quotes, stories, and powerful Scriptures, Lucinda encourages us to make life-giving and life-transforming choices on a daily basis."

—Tessa Afshar, award-winning author,
Land of Silence and *Pearl in the Sand*

"*Life-Giving Choices* captured both my mind and my heart on every page. A consummate storyteller and woman of wisdom, Lucinda Secrest McDowell hands readers like me the practical tools we need to *live well*. This is the book you want to have on hand to give as a good gift to the people you love."

—Margot Starbuck,
author of *Not Who I Imagined:
Surprised by a Loving God*

"Though I've avoided facing certain areas of my life, through *Life-Giving Choices*, I've been reminded that God wants to walk through those paths with me. I have been blessed and given hope that I can make a difference for His kingdom. Thank you, Cindy, for writing a book most of us women truly need!"

—Valerie Elliot Shepard,
author of *Devotedly—The Personal Letters
and Love Story of Jim and Elisabeth Elliot*

"Life is filled with opportunities to choose that ultimately determine the quality of life we enjoy. In *Life-Giving Choices,* Lucinda Secrest McDowell shares powerful personal stories and engaging reflection questions to help us untangle the choices. Each devotional is a beautiful invitation to choose God's best in every situation."

—Dr. Saundra Dalton-Smith, MD,
author of *Sacred Rest*

Our decisions determine our destinies. As you are faced with different decisions each day, *Life-Giving Choices* will help you choose well. Lucinda writes with beauty, truth, humor, and wisdom. I was greatly encouraged by this book, and I think you will be too!"

—Arlene Pellicane,
speaker and author of *Parents Rising*

Most major choices are made in the first half of life, correct? Not. At. All. As a woman in my senior years, I want to be even more intentional about using well the years that remain, which includes mentoring others behind me on the journey. I am ever so thankful for Lucinda Secrest McDowell's beautifully enriching guide that empowers readers of all ages to decide each day how to handle what comes our way.

—Maggie Wallem Rowe,
author of *This Life We Share:*
Journeying Well with God and Others

"In her latest book, *Life-Giving Choices*, author Lucinda Secrest McDowell gives us a precious gift. Her insight, gleaned from the foundation of God's Word, reminds us that a life well-lived is a series of conscious choices. Written in her engaging style and sprinkled with personal stories and anecdotes, this volume encourages believers to reach for God's best with every decision we make. This book will have a permanent home on my favorites shelf, and I'll keep extras to share with others."

—Edie Melson,
award-winning author and director
of the Blue Ridge Mountains Christian
Writers Conference

for Cyndi –
Choose wisely!

Life-Giving Choices

60 Days to What Matters Most

Deuteronomy 30.19

Lucinda Secrest McDowell

Lucinda Secrest McDowell

NEW HOPE®
PUBLISHERS
Imprint of Iron Stream Media
Birmingham, AL

New Hope® Publishers
100 Missionary Ridge
Birmingham, AL 35242
NewHopePublishers.com
An imprint of Iron Stream Media
IronStreamMedia.com

New Hope Publishers serves its authors as they express their views, which may not express the views of the publisher.

Library of Congress Cataloging-in-Publication Data

Names: McDowell, Lucinda Secrest, 1953- author.
Title: Life-giving choices : 60 days to what matters most / Lucinda Secrest McDowell.
Description: Birmingham : New Hope Publishers, 2019. | Includes bibliographical references.
Identifiers: LCCN 2019022592 (print) | LCCN 2019022593 (ebook) | ISBN 9781563092794 (trade paperback) | ISBN 9781563092800 (ebook)
Subjects: LCSH: Christian women—Religious life—Prayers and devotions. | Choices—Religious aspects—Christianity—Prayers and devotions.
Classification: LCC BV4527 .M389 2019 (print) | LCC BV4527 (ebook) | DDC 242/.643—dc23 LC record available at https://lccn.loc.gov/2019022592 LC ebook record available at https://lccn.loc.gov/2019022593

Copyright information continues on p. 205.

Italics in Scripture quotations reflect the author's added emphasis.

ISBN-13: 978-1-56309-279-4
Ebook ISBN: 978-1-56309-280-0

1 2 3 4 5—23 22 21 20 19

Dedicated to Mama—Sarah Hasty Secrest

Thank you for life, love, prayers, and for giving me the courage
and confidence to choose wisely.

Today I have given you the choice between life and death, between
blessings and curses. Now I call on heaven and earth to witness the choice
you make. Oh, that you would choose life . . . You can make this choice by
loving the LORD your God, obeying him, and committing yourself firmly to
him. This is the key to your life. —Deuteronomy 30:19–20

*T*he great danger facing all of us . . . is not that we shall make an absolute failure of life, nor that we shall fall into outright viciousness, nor that we shall be terribly unhappy, nor that we shall feel that life has no meaning at all—not these things. The danger is that we may fail to perceive life's greatest meaning, fall short of its highest good, miss its deepest and most abiding happiness, be unable to render the most needed service, be unconscious of life ablaze with the light of the Presence of God—and be content to have it so—that is the danger. . . . That is what one prays one's friends may be spared—satisfaction with life that falls short of the best. —Phillips Brooks (1835–1893)[1]

Contents

Day 1

Choose What Matters Most

But now let me show you a way of life that is best of all.

—1 Corinthians 12:31

All the things. Good things. Worthy things. Extraordinary people, adventurous journeys, breathtaking beauty, life-changing words, fulfilling service, quiet moments, and soul-stretching creativity.

But how do I *choose?*

My own life is full of obligation, deadlines, hurry, complicated relationships, overdue bills, medical challenges, juggling jobs—all seasoned with occasional bouts of guilt and insecurity. Because I can't *do* it all. I can't *be* it all. Too often choices are already made for me in the flash of a need to be filled or a last-minute request granted.

I tell myself, "It's all good." And, for the most part, it is. I am not struggling between the lesser of two evils; more often I'm struggling between two equally good things. My challenge is how to distinguish what matters most.

The Apostle Paul wrote that God offers a path that brings life to us and allows us to pursue that which works to enlarge and enrich our existence rather than diminish or crush our spirit. In the verses following today's Scripture passage, he spends all of 1 Corinthians 13 defining love, which characterizes the "way of life that is best of all." Love is essential and life-giving. Love is what matters most. "For I want you to *understand what really matters*, so that you may live pure and blameless lives until the day of Christ's return" (Philippians 1:10).

We can choose.

It is actually within our power to decide each day *how* we will live out the numerous interruptions, joys, crises, and surprises that come our way as twenty-first century women. With endless resources provided by the One who knows us best and loves us most—God, the creator and sustainer of the universe.

When I feel all alone in my secret struggles, I can *choose connection* instead of isolation. When headlines are frightening, I can *choose courage* instead of fear. When people break my heart, I can *choose healing* instead of despair. And when the world is simply a cacophony of chaos, I can *choose silence, calm*, and *serenity*.

Are you ready to choose what matters most?

For those tired of living the way you always have, you can start right here, right now!

> We want life to have meaning, we want fulfillment, healing and even ecstasy, but the human paradox is that we find these things by starting where we are. . . . We must look for blessings to come from unlikely, everyday places.[1]

But there is a caveat—every time we say *yes* to one choice, we must inevitably say *no* to something else. Nothing good ever comes easy. Are you ready to sacrifice? To let go of much in order to embrace *less*? To relinquish productivity in order to *rest*? To break down the polished, filtered, public façade in order to live with *authenticity*?

Author Emily P. Freeman urges that instead of striving to make the perfect choice, we should attempt to discern whether a potential decision is "life-draining" or "life-giving." She says, "Close your eyes, open one hand in your lap and put the other on your heart, and ask yourself, *What am I longing for in this moment? What is life-giving?* . . . No matter the choice you make today or in the future, Jesus is with you. He has gone before you. And he will remain with you no matter the result."[2]

For the next sixty days let's take our ordinary lives and discover a few of the amazing life-giving choices available to each of us. As we venture into new opportunities and embrace grace, Jesus will help us become life-givers of healing and hope to a broken world.

> *Lord, I give up. I'm tired of trying to do all and be all, only to end up disappointing everyone, myself, and, I feel, even You. Will You help me begin to intentionally make choices for life through Your Word and Your way? Starting today, and through Holy Spirit power, I begin. Amen.*

How Will I Choose What Matters Most?

Pray for discernment and guidance in all things.

Choose Hope

Grab the promised hope with both hands and never let go. It's an unbreakable spiritual lifeline, reaching past all appearances right to the very presence of God.

—Hebrews 6:18–19 *The Message*

I was in danger of drowning and needed a lifeline.

We were six twentysomethings all strapped to a large earth-mover inner tube riding the whitewater rapids of the Nantahala River. I know, crazy. Did I mention we were only in our twenties?

We hit a rock, I lost my grip, and I plopped down into the foaming water. When I heard one guy say, "We can't wait for her," I stopped flailing and miraculously hauled myself up several feet (in wet blue jeans) to the top of the inner tube to grab hold and never let go!

Hope is like that. It's an "unbreakable spiritual lifeline . . . right to the very presence of God." One we desperately need in our lives today because whether or not we realize it, the whitewater is swirling, and companions aren't always dependable.

Some feel with all the discord in the world today we have no obvious reason to be people of hope. But our Scripture passage from today also says hope reaches "past all appearances"—it is unseen but very present.

I've included today's text in *The Message* translation by Eugene Peterson who in 2018 went home to the Lord—a man of peace and hope until the very end. I liked Beth Moore's Tweet at the time of his death, "Don't you just sorta hope when Eugene Peterson finally sees the gorgeous, glorious face of the Savior he has so long loved and served, that Jesus is the type that might greet him with something from *The Message* translation? Like, maybe John 21:12 'Breakfast is ready.'"

Peterson knew the faithfulness of his God through eight decades of life and therefore chose to put his hope on the line every single day. He said, "I don't know one thing about the future. I don't know what the next hour will hold. . . . Still, despite my ignorance and surrounded by tinny optimists and cowardly pessimists, I say that God will accomplish his will, and I cheerfully persist in living in the hope that nothing will separate me from Christ's love."[1]

Will you choose to be a person of hope today? Despite any doom and gloom that may surround you? Despite circumstances that point to hopelessness?

Choice is a powerful weapon against the naysayers of the world, against the evil of the world.

Viktor E. Frankl wrote about his own choices as an inmate in Auschwitz concentration camp during World War II in his book *Man's Search for Meaning*. He believed prisoners who concentrated on their purpose for life fared better than those without hope. He said, "Everything can be taken from a man but one thing: the last of the human freedoms—to choose one's attitude in any given set of circumstances, to choose one's own way."[2]

The truth is we all have reason to hope in the future if we are basing our hope in God, the creator and sustainer of the universe. He is never caught by surprise with the conditions of our society and the results of our widening chasm.

As people of hope, both our words and actions must be centered in confidence and courage.

> Hoping does not mean doing nothing. . . . It is the opposite of desperate and panicky manipulations, of scurrying and worrying. And hoping is not dreaming. It is not spinning an illusion or fantasy to protect us from our boredom or our pain. It means a confident, alert expectation that God will do what he said he will do. It is imagination put in the harness of faith. It is a willingness to let him do it his way and in his time. It is the opposite of making plans that we demand that God put into effect, telling him both how and when to do it. —Eugene Peterson, *A Long Obedience in the Same Direction: Discipleship in an Instant Society*[3]

May we overflow with hope today. "Oh! May the God of green hope fill you up with joy, fill you up with peace, so that your believing lives, filled with the life-giving energy of the Holy Spirit, will brim over with hope!" (Romans 15:13 *The Message*).

Lord, You know how I struggle with being hopeful every time I'm faced with a seemingly hopeless situation. Please reach down to me today and lift me up—be my God of green and living hope. Amen.

How Will I Choose Hope?

_____

_____

_____

_____

_____

_____

$\mathcal{D}\mathcal{A}\mathcal{Y}\ 3$

Choose Authenticity

We now have this light shining in our hearts, but we ourselves are like fragile clay jars containing this great treasure. This makes it clear that our great power is from God, not from ourselves.

—2 Corinthians 4:7

*I*t was only half a tooth. But it was half of my *front* tooth—and it had broken off completely.

When I looked in the mirror, a shocked and snaggletoothed woman stared back at me. I numbly finished combing my hair and walked downstairs to where my weekend hostess had breakfast waiting. In the quiet of her beautiful Victorian seaside home, I burst into tears.

My looming fear was that my front tooth could never be fixed or we couldn't afford to replace it—and I would always look this way. Then a secondary dread emerged . . . I had to speak to hundreds of women today! The entire day. And a videographer had already been procured to capture my lectures on film.

I had become Exhibit A of brokenness on display for the entire world to see.

Friends, it's moments like these when all the insecurity and vulnerability of even the most seasoned professional speaker kick in. First, I deliberated on opening with an elaborate funny story of "what happened on my way to the women's conference." Then I considered using it as an illustration of my third presentation, entitled (Are you ready?) "Brokenness."

But I wasn't feeling especially jovial, and I realized immediately that a broken front tooth is hardly a blip for so many people who are truly suffering and broken. So I finally chose a third path.

I spent the whole conference wearing bright coral lipstick speaking and laughing and chatting with women, never once acknowledging the obvious wide gap in the middle of my face.

And God showed up.

Because I quite simply *got over myself* and focused on the business at hand—encouraging, teaching, and challenging hungry and hurting women. By the end of the day, we had become so saturated in the sweet Spirit of Jesus, that it was time to draw strength for the charge of going forth into our own homes, our own little worlds from the overflow of a filled soul.

I concluded, "And so, you now have a choice—will you risk everything for a life of adventure in the presence, power, and purpose of God? Or will you play it safe, doing the same thing with the same predictable and limiting results? This morning when I broke my front tooth, I had a choice to either allow that to totally sidetrack my mission and message or to move forward—imperfectly—in what I *do* have to offer you. I am so glad I didn't end up falling into the trap of *making it all about me*. Thank you for your grace and generosity. My prayer is when you too show up with nothing much but pure obedience, the world will listen and love you as well."

What was essential that Saturday was the women who came and the message God gave. The lovely decorations weren't all that important. The outstanding acoustics and expert videographer were not even the focus. And most certainly how the guest speaker looked was the least significant thing of all!

The next time something breaks in your life just as you are about to embark on kingdom work, will you choose to recognize it for what it is—a temptation to get sidetracked, get rattled, or give up? Don't give in. Because you and I are simply the vessels of the treasure deep inside. The light will shine through the cracks.

Lord, sometimes I'm tempted to hide behind a mask instead of showing my true self. Please help me to allow Your light and strength to shine through my cracks. Through You I can be real. Amen.

How Will I Choose Authenticity?

_____

_____

_____

_____

_____

_____

_____

_____

_____

_____

_____

_____

_____

_____

_____

_____

_____

_____

Day 4

Choose Silence

This is what the Sovereign LORD, the Holy One of Israel, says: "Only in returning to me and resting in me will you be saved. In quietness and confidence is your strength. But you would have none of it."

—Isaiah 30:15

This week I ran away from home.

I ran away from the endless noise of ringing phones and television; the constant responsibility of laundry, meals, and bills; the high piles of deskwork; and even the lovely interruptions from my sweet husband. In other words, I ran away from my life.

My birthday gift to myself was three silent days on the shore at a spiritual retreat center aptly named Mercy by the Sea.

Silence to calm and quiet my soul. Silence to think and remember. Silence to hear the voice of God.

I almost wept when I checked into my room containing a simple bed and chair facing an early spring view of lawn, daffodils, and the ocean. A perfect setting for my own triduum of mercy with no spoken words, no music, no sounds whatsoever. Except for pouring rain, singing birds, and the lapping waves. My simple meals were consumed alone—each bite a thank-you prayer for not having to plan, cook, or clean.

The first day I followed retreat materials on hope and used my own prayer book, immersing myself in the Book of Psalms. I confess I came with an agenda—I was hoping God would show me how to fix my life. But as one pastor says, "There is nothing you need to do here. . . . [Silence] can form your life even if it doesn't solve your life."[1]

Soon I realized it was far better to simply experience each moment with an open mind and open heart to what might be revealed.

Are you in need of silence today? Is it time to pull away a bit, even if only for an hour?

The rest of the world (and my family) functioned just fine without me for seventy-two hours, which was both a sobering thought and a huge relief. I mostly unplugged and left a vacation response on my email—realizing technology may be the last hardest barrier to our retreat from noise, because it represents connection.

> We don't need to respond to every word and request that comes our way. . . . Silence offers a way of paying attention to the Spirit of God and what he brings to the surface of our souls. . . . And as the silence settles in and nothing seems to be happening, we often struggle with the feeling that we are wasting time. . . . Like a can opener, the silence opens up the contents of our heart, allowing us deeper access to God than we experience at other times. As we remain in the silence, the inner noise and chaos will begin to settle. Our capacity to open up wider and wider to God grows. —Adele Calhoun, *Spiritual Disciplines Handbook: Practices That Transform Us*[2]

Where can you find pockets of silence periodically?

Most of us can't run away from our lives for three full days, but we can intentionally seek out opportunities to be quiet and reconnect with God. Whether we do a childcare exchange for an afternoon or visit a local monastery or convent for the day, our choice to come apart for a while will reap great benefits. Both to our own souls (more calm and settled) and through the spillover to all those around us.

Lord, I am surrounded by a world of noise that seems over-
whelming at times. I long for a respite of quiet and calm. Please
help me make quiet time a priority and provide a way for silence
to become part of my life. Amen.

How Will I Choose Silence?

_____

_____

_____

_____

_____

_____

_____

_____

_____

_____

_____

_____

_____

_____

_____

DAY 5

Choose Healing

> O LORD, if you heal me, I will be truly healed; if you save me, I will be truly saved. My praises are for you alone!
>
> —Jeremiah 17:14

She was so bent over her only view was the ground. Folded in half, she somehow managed to make her way through life. But imagine never looking anyone in the eye or lifting a face to the sunshine or taking in the beauty of the sky! This affliction had robbed her of so much. She had become expendable and invisible.

But Jesus saw her.

And with a word, "Dear woman, you are healed of your sickness!" she was made straight and whole. Immediately she began to praise and glorify God.

> He saw a woman who had been crippled by an evil spirit. She had been bent double for eighteen years and was unable to stand up straight. When Jesus saw her, he called her over and said, "Dear woman, you are healed of your sickness!"
>
> —Luke 13:11–12

This woman knew her burden was no easily healed malady but was a crippling condition by emotional and spiritual forces Jesus attributed to Satan—"held in bondage by Satan" (v. 16).

We aren't told the cause of her bondage. Perhaps she had sinned so grievously she was paralyzed by regret and remorse. Maybe she had been the victim of shaming, eventually succumbing to the lies telling her she was a bad person. She might have been verbally abused, even from childhood, told she was worth nothing—a constant barrage to her self-esteem.

Even if the precipitating factor had been her own choice to sin, this woman could have received complete forgiveness after confession. But perhaps, even then, she simply could not forgive herself. Without such freedom, oppression seeps into the body, and we become physiologically affected by spiritual pain.

Are you bowed low? Held back from living fully because of an oppressive spirit that impedes your mind and heart from embracing all God has for you?

It's time to make a choice. For healing.

This woman had to choose to leave her shadow existence and walk painfully toward a place of potential help. For her it was the synagogue—where the faithful gathered. Surely she would find someone with delivering power.

Jesus. Whose healing actions brought about a variety of responses. Yes, the woman was thrilled and thankful. The gathering crowds? Not so much. To them, the fact Jesus had the audacity to heal on the Sabbath was far more shocking than seeing a fellow human released from great pain and distress.

Even good stuff sometimes brings about bad press. That's why it's so important to respond to spiritual nudges despite our fear and hesitation. You too can be free today. Why not make your way to the Master? Any time works for Him—His schedule is wide open. For you.

Lord, I confess I too feel burdened by the weight of oppression, guilt, and shame. But I know this is not the way You intend for me to live. Please help me take one step toward You and Your healing today. Amen.

How Will I Choose Healing?

_____

_____

_____

_____

_____

_____

_____

_____

_____

_____

_____

_____

_____

_____

_____

_____

_____

_____

_____

_____

_____

_____

Choose Risk

Welcome [Epaphroditus] in the Lord's love and with great joy, and give him the honor that people like him deserve. For he risked his life for the work of Christ, and he was at the point of death while doing for me what you couldn't do from far away.

—Philippians 2:29–30

Why would a young widow take her toddler daughter to live deep in the South American jungle among the very same people who had speared her husband to death?

That is the question I personally asked Elisabeth Elliot so many years ago when I lived in her home as a young seminarian. In exchange for room and board, I typed manuscripts and did a bit of housecleaning—which occasionally included dusting the fierce Waorani spears propped in the corner of the living room!

As I recall, she answered me in her clear, straightforward manner. *God called me to take the gospel message to the Waorani. So when the opportunity arose, I followed obediently.*

Risky? You bet! But Elisabeth Elliot believed there was no need for faith without a conscious element of risk.

Yet how do you know *when* to take a risk? Back in the 1950s, many people warned Elisabeth not to go live in the jungle. But she held firm. "Some told me point-blank that I must be mistaken. . . . I knew that my position was quite indefensible. But I knew, too, that it was the duty which lay before me. That duty I took to be the will of God."[1]

Over the next two years of living with the Waorani in the Ecuadorian jungle, God had plenty of opportunity to both confirm His call on Elisabeth's life and also eventually redirect her to further avenues of ministry.

Is God calling you to move forward into the unknown? As you study His Word and seek godly counsel, are you willing to live with risk?

> I found peace in the knowledge that I was in the hands of God. Not in the confidence that I was not going to be killed. Not in any false sense of security that God would protect me, any more than He protected my husband . . . Simply in knowing that He held my destiny in His two hands, and that what He did was right. —Elisabeth Elliot, *The Savage My Kinsman*[2]

Truth is, life is ever so much easier when we just sit on the couch. When we keep doing the same thing over and over again getting the same results. But who wants to live a life where nothing ever changes? Why *not* take a risk when we know we have the King of the universe on our side?

I love the promise, "No eye has seen, no ear has heard, and no mind has imagined what God has prepared for those who love him" (1 Corinthians 2:9). This is the same Paul who praised Epaphroditus in today's text for being willing to risk his life.

What God has planned for you is probably more amazing than you could ever imagine, but to live it requires a strong element of faith.

> We are all climbing our own versions of Mount Everest and have no idea if our oxygen will last or if an avalanche will come, but God does. We can never underestimate the grace and the strength he will give us for whatever he is calling us to do and whatever challenges we'll face. . . . It's not about having all the right answers. . . . It's knowing that He who has called us is faithful. —Melanie Shankle, *Church of the Small Things: The Million Little Pieces That Make Up a Life*[3]

When William Wallace, as portrayed in the film *Braveheart*, rallied ordinary people in the First War of Scottish Independence from England, he helped them discover strength they never knew they had. At the Battle of Stirling, many of those farmers and villagers were afraid, but Wallace cheered them on toward victory:

> Fight, and you may die. Run, and you'll live . . . at least a while. And dying in your beds many years from now, would you be willing to trade all the days from this day to that for one chance—just one chance—to come back here and tell our enemies that they may take our lives, but they'll never take our *freedom*? —*Braveheart*, screenplay by Randall Wallace, directed by Mel Gibson

Is it time to put your life on the line?

Lord, I confess that while I'm tired of doing the same things with the same old results, I'm not sure I'm brave enough to change, to dare, to risk. Will You give me the confidence to trust You enough to obey that uneasy call? Amen.

How Will I Choose Risk?

_____

_____

_____

_____

_____

_____

Choose to Listen

Pay close attention to what you hear. The closer you listen, the more understanding you will be given—and you will receive even more.

—Mark 4:24

After a lovely dinner with old friends, my husband turned to me, "Cindy, you hardly let me get a word in all night!"

His comment took me by surprise. Had I really dominated the conversation so much? Oh dear. These *were* my former colleagues whom I hadn't seen in more than thirty years. "Oh, honey, I'm so sorry. I totally got carried away with all the catching up," I feebly mumbled.

My apology sounded lame even to me.

The truth? I talk too much and listen too little. There are consequences for that—and I'm not just talking about inadvertently shutting down my husband, awful as that was. Our Scripture passage today says, "The closer you listen, the more understanding you will be given." What we receive by keeping our mouths closed is to finally understand even more!

In my defense, I'm not the only culprit here. National Public Radio recently had an entire radio program on civility—primarily the lack of it in today's culture. One expert said the best way for each of us to help remedy this is to *listen* and look for *places of connection*. That means active listening instead of mentally preparing your own comeback while the other person is talking.

Did I strike a chord there? Are you, like me, occasionally more concerned with what you are about to say than what is being said to you at the time? Doesn't this come just a bit too close to loving the sound of our own voices?

One wise woman believes we are too deeply embedded in a culture that lunges for the microphone. She said, "We value making our voices heard and getting our points across. But if our goal is healthy community and loving our neighbors, we need to rethink our approach. . . . Only as we engage in the hidden practice of listening do we learn about the struggles of others, gaining empathy where we once cast judgment."[1]

What happens when we choose to listen—to our children, to that person who is quite different from us, to that competitive colleague, or to that needy neighbor? My own experience is that as I prayerfully close my mouth and ask God to help me see beyond the obvious words and actions into the soul, He does just that. While listening I become more compassionate, and even if I eventually leave the conversation still disagreeing with the person or still not understanding them, I am at least responding with civility.

That night my sweet husband clearly called me out on behavior that crushed his spirit, and it prompted within me a desire to prove I could indeed shut my mouth and open my ears and heart. The next day we had lunch with this same visiting couple, and I was able to focus on everyone in the group, making deliberate choices to listen more intently.

Henri Nouwen observes, "Listening is a form of spiritual hospitality by which you invite strangers to become friends."[2]

I can't think of anything more needed in our world today than the spiritual hospitality of listening. People are so hungry to be heard they pay lots of money to those who will sit and listen to their problems, their struggles, their questions. Sometimes professional therapy is necessary, but more often folks just need a person who is willing to embrace connection.

How will you choose spiritual hospitality today?

Lord, please shut my mouth and open my ears and heart. Help me be intentional about listening to the words spoken and the words hidden. May this be a path of hospitality to all I encounter, especially those who are different from me. Amen.

How Will I Choose to Listen?

_____

_____

_____

_____

_____

_____

_____

_____

_____

_____

_____

_____

_____

_____

_____

_____

_____

DAY 8

Choose Fearless

Don't be afraid, for I am with you. Don't be discouraged, for I am
your God. I will strengthen you and help you. I will hold you up with
my victorious right hand.

—Isaiah 41:10

People often say the young are fearless, totally oblivious to all the dangers and risks out there. Not me. While I didn't live in constant fear as a young adult, I had a healthy regard for danger.

For instance, while living alone in a small apartment near San Francisco, this country gal bristled at all sorts of sounds during the night. I remember being awakened more than once, thinking I had heard someone breaking in. My legs shook uncontrollably, and my heart beat quickly. It was only prayer that got me to calm down—that and constant recitation of Scripture promises.

After I married and became a mama, my greatest fears always concerned my husband or children. I didn't "borrow trouble," but I did occasionally jump to conclusions when curfews were broken or accidents happened. It took a lot to develop enough trust that I could actually sleep through the night after all my little birds flew the nest and began their own adventures out in the world.

Women often share their common fears with me—random violence, failing health, financial needs, environmental instability, and their children's futures.

Fear is a healthy emotion. God hardwired a response into our bodies to direct us to fight or flight when danger comes. But fear can turn into an unhealthy emotion if we become fearful in the face of that which is not actually dangerous, like the "what ifs" of life—those times when fear paralyzes instead of motivates because it attaches to what does not truly threaten us.

Do you find yourself worried and anxious about many things that never actually come to pass? Would you like to live without fear of the future?

Friend, we can *choose* to be fearless.

God's Word contains many verses that offer some version of "fear not." I suspect He kept repeating Himself because He knows what a problem fear can be for some of us.

How does one choose to be fearless?

Be assured of God's constant presence in hard times.

Do not be afraid, for I have ransomed you. I have called you by name; you are mine. When you go through deep waters, I will be with you. When you go through rivers of difficulty, you will not drown. When you walk through the fire of oppression, you will not be burned up; the flames will not consume you. —Isaiah 43:1–2

Trust God is stronger than anything the enemy can send your way.

But you belong to God, my dear children. You have already won a victory over those people, because the Spirit who lives in you is greater than the spirit who lives in the world. —1 John 4:4

Wear God's armor to fight life's battles.

Put on all of God's armor so that you will be able to stand firm against all strategies of the devil . . . Stand your ground, putting on the belt of truth and the body armor of God's righteousness. For shoes, put on the peace that comes from the Good News so that you will be fully prepared. In addition to all of these, hold up the shield of faith to stop the fiery arrows of the devil. Put on salvation as your helmet, and take the sword of the Spirit, which is the word of God. —Ephesians 6:11, 14–17

See yourself as a courageous warrior princess.

So be strong and courageous! Do not be afraid and do not panic before them. For the LORD your God will personally go ahead of you. He will neither fail you nor abandon you. —Deuteronomy 31:6

[Fear] will always knock on the door. Just don't invite it in for dinner, and for heaven's sake don't offer it a bed for the night. —Max Lucado, *Fearless: Imagine Your Life Without Fear*[1]

You've got this, girlfriend!

Lord, I confess I still get frightened, even though I know better. Thank You for continuing to be the Abba Father who reaches to hold my hand and guide me through any peril, real or imagined. Amen.

How Will I Choose Fearless?

_____

_____

_____

_____

_____

_____

_____

_____

DAY 9

Choose Trust

Trust in the LORD with all your heart; do not depend on your own understanding. Seek his will in all you do, and he will show you which path to take.

—Proverbs 3:5–6

The view from the porch is beautiful at Honeysuckle Farm. But on this day, thick early morning fog hides the large flowering camellia bush, majestic pine trees, and rustic guest cottage across the way.

I *know* they are there somewhere . . . but they are unseen for a moment.

As I sip the strong, hot coffee that is to be my fuel for the day ahead, Aunt Carol observes, "Cindy, this fog is like your life today. You are wondering what's ahead for your mother as she lies in the hospital recovering from surgery, sick with the flu, and facing another surgery in a few days. There are so many decisions to make, and yet nothing is clear."

Unseen for now. I gulp, realizing I am literally in a fog on how to help my frail and fragile ninety-one-year-old mama.

When I returned to my hometown, did I revert to childhood? Perhaps that's why I kept looking around for the adult in the room. The one who knew what to do, who would make wise decisions to move us forward on the caring, healing path. To my astonishment I remembered, *that person is me!*

And in the midst of the mental fog an esteemed psychologist told me, "The sign of mental health is the ability to handle ambiguity." What is ambiguity? Being able to say, "I know that I don't know, and that's okay."

I wondered if I could handle this not knowing, this *fog*.

Aunt Carol is one of the wisest women I know. How grateful I was to nestle under her afghan (which she *knitted* with yarn she *spun* from sheep she *raised*) and hear these next words: "The fog will lift, Cindy, and all will be made clear. One step at a time. God will show you what needs to be done and when. Trust Him with your precious mama."

Almost two weeks ensued—some days clear, others cloudy. Small steps, big steps. Transition from hospital to rehab, and then it was time for me to fly home. Even though Mama was *not yet healed*.

My final morning coffee with Aunt Carol was yet again shrouded in deep fog.

"This is a journey," she said. "None of us knows what the future holds, even today. Remember your mama has a strong will and desire to recover and live. I know my sister, and she is not afraid. You can truly leave her in God's hands."

What I desire for my sweet mama is peace, not pain. But I had to return home feeling helpless and too far away, though grateful Jesus is still by her side, breaking through every foggy barrier and bringing His light.

I can definitely relate to those disciples who had a hard time understanding what was going on in the upper room, prompting Jesus to say, "You don't understand now what I am doing, but someday you will" (John 13:7).

Emotionally and physically exhausted from my time caring for my mother, I almost regretted that on my first day home I had volunteered to run the book table at a conference where my husband was the emcee. Yet I smiled upon reading the title of the guest speaker's book—*Becoming a Healing Presence.* Can you even imagine how much his words ministered to me that day? They were life-giving and timely.

I'm trying to accept this season of concern about my mother's compromised health. Of living with ambiguity as I pray daily for God's provision, power, and peace in her life.

Do you find yourself in a fog today? Are you faced with a major decision? A conflicted relationship?

In the midst of a life fog as thick as pea soup, why not choose these affirmations that our retreat speaker, Dr. Albert Rossi, shared for traveling the path of trust toward patience and peace:

> I know that I don't know.
> I know that Christ knows.
> I trust Him.
>
> —Dr. Albert S. Rossi,
> author of *Becoming a Healing Presence*

Lord, I feel so helpless when I can't see what is ahead. Help me learn to live with situations out of my control. May I trust You for each decision and provision, for You are truly worthy. Amen.

How Will I Choose Trust?

_____

_____

_____

_____

_____

_____

_____

_____

_____

_____

Day 10

Choose to Encourage

So encourage each other and build each other up, just as you are
already doing.

—1 Thessalonians 5:11

As a child he was called Fat Freddy.

The other kids bullied and viciously mocked him. To combat the loneliness he often felt, Freddy used stuffed animals and puppets to create whole new worlds in his bedroom. Places of safety and acceptance. And he determined that "victim" would not define his life. He would be sensitive to the pain of others—seek to build them up rather than crush them down.

When a young Fred finished seminary in the early 1960s he felt a strong calling to encourage children and was "ordained in the ministry of television."[1] He went on to host *Mister Rogers' Neighborhood,* which aired for thirty-three years to both great acclaim and occasional criticism.

But when public television was in danger of being abolished in the late 1960s, Mr. Rogers's testimony before a US Senate subcommittee helped keep the Public Broadcasting System going. I can't even imagine today without PBS!

Fred Rogers was a pioneer in emphasizing that the feelings of young children are as important as those of adults. He championed human dignity for all and the value of unconditional love. He was a musician, and in the documentary, "Won't You Be My Neighbor," he sits at his piano and describes his work as "[helping] children through some of the difficult modulations of life."

How can you encourage someone? Listen to them and affirm their worth. Speak into their lives with words of affirmation and empowerment.

Fred Rogers believed:

> The greatest thing that we can do is to help somebody know that they're loved and capable of loving.
>
> As human beings our job in life is to help people realize how rare and valuable each one of us really is, that each of us has something that no one else has—or ever will have—something inside that is unique to all time.
>
> To love someone is to strive to accept that person exactly the way he or she is, right here and now.[2]

Words can build us up or tear us down. I've been the recipient of words that heal and words that crush. Sadly, I've also been the one speaking both kinds of words.

But I determined the next time I found myself frustrated and critical about someone's behavior, I would ask God to show me the story behind the story and give me words to touch that part of them (and not just the obnoxious part that was acting out). I always utter a prayer because it takes spiritual insight to recognize the defense mechanisms people so often put up for survival.

And yet, in the very act of seeing a person's struggle, we are in a perfect position to encourage them beyond it.

Do you find it easier to encourage or to criticize? While it is true various personalities are often either more optimistic or more pessimistic, we do not have to be ruled by our wiring or our mood. We can freely choose the words we use on other people. And if encouragement isn't our default, we can choose to change.

Some people say Mr. Rogers went overboard by convincing a whole generation of children they were special. And yes, there probably is a fine line between growing up feeling special and growing up feeling entitled. But I believe the deciding factor lies in the intent. By encouraging others to be all God created them to be, we can be used to help draw out the gifts and potential that have possibly been overlooked or even squelched. One journalist noted, "When Mr. Rogers called you special, it didn't feel like entitlement or mindless praise. It felt more like a responsibility—like he was reminding you to live up to something. And even when you didn't live up to it, he was still there with those simple words that, even now, carry an awful lot of emotional heft: 'I like you just the way you are.'"[3]

One of Mister Rogers's favorite songs to sing to his young audiences was *It's You I Like.* The lyrics reiterate that the listening child is liked not because of the way he looks or what he accomplishes or even how he feels on any given day. What Mister Rogers is singing is that each child is liked unconditionally, just as he is. What a message we all need to hear every day.

Sounds like loving encouragement to me.

> *Lord, when someone notices my potential and prods me to reach it, I smile all over. May I be that kind of encourager to all I encounter today, beginning with those I know best—the ones in my own home and circle. Amen.*

How Will I Choose to Encourage?

_____

_____

_____

_____

_____

_____

Choose Gratitude

Be thankful in all circumstances, for this is God's will for you who belong to Christ Jesus.

—1 Thessalonians 5:18

Australian novelist Morris West suggests that at a certain age our lives simplify and we need have only three phrases left in our spiritual vocabulary: "Thank you! Thank you! Thank you!"

English minister John Henry Jowett once observed, "Gratitude is a vaccine, an antitoxin, and an antiseptic." What better cure for what ails society today—choosing to have a grateful heart!

Who knew? For a long time, gratitude wasn't even listed in the *Encyclopedia of Human Emotions*, a standard psychology text. Today, new studies by social scientists reveal what others have taught for centuries—gratitude is an indispensable demonstration of virtue and an integral component to living strong.

> Gratitude reaches down into our very souls and awakens the slumbering feelings of grace and love we have for one another. "If you concentrate on finding whatever is good in every situation," says Rabbi Harold Kushner, "you will discover that your life will suddenly be filled with gratitude, a feeling that nurtures the soul." —Les Parrott, *You're Stronger Than You Think: The Power to Do What You Feel You Can't*[1]

Is your own soul overflowing with gratitude? If not, why not?

Perhaps it's easier to whine about what's gone wrong. Or to never intentionally notice all that has been already received. During Christmas, a short video aimed at the commercialization of the holidays went viral. In it a man awakens wrapped as a package and thanks God for the gift of life. Then he looks down and sees his feet wrapped up and thanks God for shoes. His kids come running in covered in wrapping paper and he thanks God for his family. Well, you get the idea—we already have so many gifts for which to be thankful! But are we grateful for them?

What will you thank God for today? "Whatever is good and perfect is a gift coming down to us from God our Father, who created all the lights in the heavens. He never changes or casts a shifting shadow" (James 1:17). He is, after all, the one we thank. Sadly, many people do not believe this. "The worst moment for an atheist is when he is really thankful and has no one to thank," wrote G. K. Chesterton.

Anyone can grow a grateful heart with practice. Just decide that you will try to follow the biblical command to "always be thankful" (Colossians 3:15). If you can't be thankful for what happened, be grateful for God's provision of His presence and peace in the midst of whatever happened.

One godly man who has lived long enough to recognize the enduring qualities that define a Christ-follower believes gratitude is a tangible sign we are growing in holiness: "Gratitude not only defines sanctity, it also defines maturity. We are mature to the degree that we are grateful. . . . To be a saint is to be fueled by gratitude, nothing more and nothing less. . . . Outside of gratitude we find ourselves doing many of the right things for the wrong reasons."[2]

I'm glad I was trained from a young age to notice. I actually have a crumpled copy of a "Thankful List" I created at age twelve in which I clearly listed seventy different things I was thankful for—all in categories, no less! But now, in the autumn season of my life, I don't choose to write down that many items. My list is shorter but much deeper. Priceless gifts I notice. Every single day.

As you are growing up, don't forget to be grateful.

Lord, as George Herbert once prayed, "Thou that hast given so much to me, give one thing more,—a grateful heart." May I choose to see all of life as a gift from Your providential hand, and may I never stop thanking You. Amen.

How Will I Choose Gratitude?

_____

_____

_____

_____

_____

_____

_____

_____

_____

_____

_____

_____

_____

_____

_____

_____

_____

_____

DAY 12

Choose Obedience

And she went right off and did it, did just as Elijah asked. And it turned out as he said—daily food for her and her family. The jar of meal didn't run out and the bottle of oil didn't become empty: GOD's promise fulfilled to the letter.

—1 Kings 17:15–16 *The Message*

E lijah was tired and hungry and had been told by God where to find someone who would provide for his needs.

The woman was also tired and hungry, but in addition to that, she was a single mother who was struggling to care for her son.

So when Elijah asked her for food and drink, she tearfully replied:

I swear by the LORD your God that I don't have a single piece of bread in the house. And I have only a handful of flour left in the jar and a little cooking oil in the bottom of the jug. I was just gathering a few sticks to cook this last meal, and then my son and I will die. —v. 12

Can you tell she was desperate?

Widows were often overlooked during biblical times. If they had no grown sons to take care of them, they had no legal protection. And in a drought, as was taking place in the area the widow lived, every family was fighting to survive. Of all the people Elijah could ask for help, she does not seem to be the best choice. Only a handful of flour and a little oil stood between this poor woman and starving to death.

Though not of his faith, the widow recognized Elijah was a godly man: evident from her words "I swear by the LORD your God." She lived in Zarephath, a town inhabited by Baal worshippers. Nevertheless, God had seen something exceptional in this widow and sent Elijah to her for the sake of both the woman and the prophet.

And both of them obeyed.

If you were down to the last amount of food and drink needed to keep your child alive, would you give it away to the prophet who wanders in the door requesting it? Even if he does claim to be the voice of God?

Elijah promised if she fed him first, she would never run out of flour or oil—the Lord God would keep filling her jars until the rains came again bringing a harvest of crops. Desperate enough to risk life for God's favor, this woman is remembered in the Bible, "And she went right off and did it" (v. 15 *The Message*).

Sometimes we are to just do as God says—speaking to us through His Word, a nudge from the Holy Spirit, or godly advice from trusted counsel.

And she lived happily ever after, right? Wrong! Because soon, her son grew ill and actually died, causing her to scream and blame Elijah's God. Hadn't she done the impossible already—offered up her final provision? How could God take her child now?

Elijah immediately prayed, "O LORD my God, why have you brought tragedy to this widow who has opened her home to me, causing her son to die? . . . Please let this child's life return to him" (vv. 20–21).

And the child lived.

Is God worth our obedience, even in the toughest of times?

> There had been nothing to offer—no baked bread and no way to make it. But nothing was more than enough when it was given to a trustworthy God. Faith in God can fill jars with flour and children with breath. . . . As Elijah handed the widow's son back into her shaking arms, he whispered to her, "See? He lives." And in response, the woman nodded, knowing that it was true, that it was wonderful. —Angie Smith, *For Such a Time as This*[1]

Lord, all too often I long to see the end results before I'm ready to obey Your command. Please help me emulate this desperate widow and realize that You truly see the whole picture and will always reward obedience. Amen.

How Will I Choose Obedience?

_____

_____

_____

_____

_____

_____

_____

_____

_____

_____

_____

_____

_____

_____

_____

DAY 13

Choose Blessing

Don't retaliate with insults when people insult you. Instead, pay them back with a blessing. That is what God has called you to do, and he will grant you his blessing.

—1 Peter 3:9

Billy Graham once said that when we get to heaven, we are going to discover a whole barn full of blessings and answered prayers we never dared seek.

But I don't want to miss out on any good thing God has for me—so I keep asking and praying. *Who can I bless today?*

Twenty years ago I found myself struggling over whether or not to keep writing. "No one will miss this book if I never write it . . . " I muttered under my breath.

When my first book *Amazed by Grace* came out, I excitedly shared with an old seminary friend that I had a book published, "It's everything I know!"

She replied. "It's awfully thin."

So needless to say when a contract offer came for another book, I hesitated. Did I have anything else worth saying? Did anyone even *read* my books? Writing is both excruciating and exhilarating, and I asked God to give me a sign as to whether or not I should continue.

That very afternoon I chose to bless a stranger and found my own barn of blessings in return.

I was taking a break during a staff retreat when I wandered into the garden of the Mercy Center, encountering an old woman digging in the dirt. Wanting to encourage and affirm her, I commented, "Your flowers are beautiful. By the way, I'm Cindy."

The Sister introduced herself with an Irish lilt and explained she had been there for a one-year sabbatical and would be returning to Ireland the next week.

Already impressed with the liveliness of this elderly nun, I asked what she did while on sabbatical at the convent. "Well, for one thing we read a book a week and report on it to our spiritual director."

"So does that mean you just read fifty-two books?" I exclaimed, wishing someone would tell me I had to read a book a week. With my job, a husband, and four children, reading was still my passion though time for it was rare. But my favorite Catholic author was Henri Nouwen, so I kept talking, seeking to build a bridge.

"Sister, of all those fifty-two books, which one did you like the best?" I inquired.

"Why, that's easy," she replied with a slight twinkle in her eye. "*Amazed by Grace!*"

Immediately my jaw dropped as I looked completely dumbfounded, which caused her to conclude that perhaps I didn't like it.

"N–no, that's not it . . ." I trailed off, not trusting my voice.

She went on, "Actually, I read it twice, and it changed my life. The author is McDowell."

Finally able to speak, I blurted out, "Sister, I *wrote* that book!"

Then it was her turn to look dumbfounded with dropped jaw. This Cindy-in-the-garden-in-blue-jeans didn't look like her mental image of Lucinda-Secrest-McDowell-the-author. We laughed, hugged, and had a precious time of fellowship in the garden. A frumpy, Protestant, middle-aged mama of four and an octogenarian Irish Catholic nun both reveling in how God's grace changed our lives.

I would have totally missed that blessing if I hadn't reached out to greet and engage her. This Sister was God's sign to me that indeed He did intend to use my words for His kingdom.

I signed that new book contract, and twelve more since then.

How can you be a blessing today? It takes an intentional choice to engage.

Our true souls are seen when we reach out in love—the biblical word for this is *blessing*.

> Blessing is not just a word. Blessing is the projection of good into the life of another. We must think it, and feel it, and will it. We communicate it with our bodies. Blessing is kind of like an ancient dance of the Hokey-Pokey; before you finish you have to "put your whole self in." Blessing is done by the soul. —John Ortberg, *Soul Keeping: Caring for the Most Important Part of You*[1]

Lord, I know there are blessings indeed around every corner if I will only pay attention. Thank You for helping me reach out to offer a blessing to someone I meet, knowing that in Your sovereignty, all encounters have meaning and purpose. Amen.

How Will I Choose Blessing?

_____

_____

_____

_____

_____

_____

_____

_____

Day 14

Choose Connection

By yourself you're unprotected. With a friend you can face the worst. Can you round up a third? A three-stranded rope isn't easily snapped.

—Ecclesiastes 4:12 *The Message*

C. S. Lewis knew how important it was to have like-minded friends with similar interests and concerns. For Lewis it was those who shared the same passion for writing and creating—like J. R. R. Tolkien and Charles Williams. So the Inklings gathered together twice a week in community, out of which came such classic works as *The Screwtape Letters* and the fantasy series The Lord of the Rings. One writer said, "It is important not to overstate the importance of this group . . . now widely acclaimed as one of the greatest literary clubs of the twentieth century. . . . To challenge the status quo demands fellowship and commitment. . . . Lewis emphasized the privilege of being part of such a group. 'In a good Friendship, every member often feels humility towards the rest. He sees that they are splendid, and counts himself lucky to be among them.'"[1]

Do you have professional connections of the soul—like-minded women who "get" you?

I'm grateful for many groups of friends, not the least of which are my dear SpaSisters who offer endless counsel, wisdom, support, and prayer for me both professionally and personally. This name is really misleading because we have never communed together over a whirlpool or sauna. But we have gathered for a decade of spiritual spas, and I find I can jump right in no matter how long it has been since the last communiqué. No long explanations needed—we are all seasoned authors, speakers, and women in leadership seeking balance. They are truly sisters who know what my life is like.

A new connection with a guild of mostly younger women who are writing and speaking on cutting-edge issues is also timely for me. Every day these sisters (through our online group) teach me something new and point me to exciting ministries that are evolving in fresh wineskins. And occasionally, I'm able to offer wisdom and encouragement from my own lifetime of writing and speaking. I eagerly look forward to more.

Would you like to thrive in your own connections? Here are some guidelines I have found helpful:

Never Compare—Competition can kill connections. Recognize you both have strengths and unique stories to live. Don't try to imitate her journey or personal style. Be confident in who you are and what you have to offer.

Keep Confidences—Nothing destroys a relationship faster than revealing secrets. Be a person she can trust, whether she talks to you about her professional concerns or personal struggles.

Promote Her Publicly—Praise her publicly and recognize her contribution to your life (or even your work) when appropriate. Be a cheerleader.

Brainstorm Together—One great service we can perform with others is to listen. Then, be an authentic soundboard and *always be kind*.

Refer Her When Appropriate—Chances are you may one day be offered an opportunity that is not your forte, but fits her perfectly. How gracious if you recommend her as an even better fit.

Plan Appointments—If you are both going to be at the same event or even overlapping on a trip, plan in advance a time for one-on-one catch up if at all possible. This shows how much you value keeping in touch.

Share Her Joys—Make a deliberate effort to congratulate her on personal and professional achievements. If nobody "at home" noticed, your words will be especially appreciated.

Endorse Her Work—If asked and you are able, seek to endorse her work and recommend her to others. When speaking of her in public, be sincere in your praise.

Don't Use Her—Yes, our friends have all sorts of contacts, and while there is nothing wrong with occasionally utilizing their resources, try not to make this a habit or certainly not the basis of your relationship.

Keep Expectations Loose—She is your friend, but she is also friends with many other people. Don't expect to always be included in every gathering, and don't assume rejection when you see her social media posts.

Welcome New People—Don't always gravitate only to those you already know at gatherings, worship, or even meetings. Reach out to welcome new people into your life and expect a blessing.

Pray for Her—And by that, I mean don't just *say* you will pray for her—do it! If possible, pray over specific requests she shares with you. This may be the most important glue for your relationship. We grow to love those for whom we pray.

There is strength in connection!

Lord, I thank You for those other women who are walking similar paths and heeding similar callings on their lives as I am in mine. Please help me learn from them and be gracious to sisters at every juncture of both success and setback. May I treasure all such connections. Amen.

How Will I Choose Connection?

_____

_____

_____

_____

_____

_____

_____

_____

_____

_____

_____

_____

_____

_____

_____

_____

_____

_____

_____

_____

DAY 15

Choose Mercy

Judge fairly, and show mercy and kindness to one another. Do not oppress widows, orphans, foreigners, and the poor.

—Zechariah 7:9–10

My 1968 Ford rattled across the rickety bridge deep in the hollows of Kentucky, literally driving on a wing and a prayer. Rounding the bend, the scent hit me before I even caught sight of the Caudhills's place.

The old weathered house stood on a hill. On the porch and throughout the yard were piles and piles of old clothes that well-meaning people had donated to the family. Unfortunately, no one had bothered to sort through them—a task that bewildered the Caudhills. And so, the piles just sat there—crumpled, wet, and moldy.

As I arrived, Jim, a handsome tow-headed boy of ten, ran down to greet "Miss Cindy." Every day I took him to the nearby hollow where I directed a recreation enrichment program for the mountain children. Jim was beautiful and bright—a ray of hope amid the squalor. He lived with his mother, aunt, and uncle—all of whom had intellectual disabilities. They stood tall and formidable on the porch waving goodbye. I often wondered what they thought about my taking Jim away each day.

I was here partly due to Catherine Marshall's *Christy*—a fictional tribute to the author's mother, which I had already read three times. I wanted to be just like my heroine, Christy—to serve the rural poor with Christ's love, to bring them hope and a better life. Renting a small room from an old widow, I learned how to quilt, clear fields, wash my hair in rainwater buckets (we had no running water), use an outhouse, endure being teased as an old maid, and eat biscuits three times a day.

In that summer of my twentieth year I traipsed around Kentucky in my cutoff overalls and long braids, determined to save the world—or at least this tiny part of it in the Eastern Kentucky mountains. By the time I had returned to university in the fall to finish up my senior year, God had planted precious seeds of mercy in my heart and mind.

Their world had changed me.

God's grace stepped in and redeemed my efforts that summer. He took a young, privileged, sheltered student and opened my eyes to a world of need, softened my heart to hear His voice, and brought me to the end of myself so that I might allow God to work mercy *through* me.

At the beginning of my third decade, I slowly began to embrace what the Lord asks of all his people in Micah 6:8, "To do what is right, to love mercy, and to walk humbly with your God."

But how do I continue to extend mercy daily to widows, orphans, and the less fortunate (which is most of the world) every day? I must admit, this question haunts me. You too?

I believe it begins by *noticing,* right where we are. If we follow God's lead and walk through the open doors (no matter how scary), He will put people and situations in our path that demand a response.

At the height of the Rwandan genocide, the US Department of Justice loaned one of their young lawyers to the United Nations to direct a team gathering evidence against the perpetrators. This Harvard graduate named Gary Haugen was so changed by this experience that he founded the International Justice Mission. The mercy that stirred his heart compelled him to dedicate all his efforts to bringing immediate relief to victims of violence and oppression around the world and to pursuing prosecution of perpetrators who abuse power to violate and suppress the weak—"the least of these."

Mercy costs us. What will it cost you and me today to show mercy and kindness to one another?

Lord, I shudder to think where I would be without the generous mercy You bestow on me every day. My response is to seek to do what is right, love mercy, and walk humbly with You. May that always include reaching out to the most unfortunate among us. Amen.

How Will I Choose Mercy?

_____

_____

_____

_____

_____

_____

_____

_____

_____

_____

_____

_____

_____

_____

_____

_____

Choose Release

He has sent me to comfort the brokenhearted and to proclaim that
captives will be released and prisoners will be freed.

—Isaiah 61:1

Like thousands around the world, I prayed for my former neighbor
Andrew Brunson while he was convicted on terror charges and imprisoned in Turkey for two years.

And then, after years of negotiations, he was released. Against all odds.

Looking at a potential lengthy jail sentence, in an interview with VOA
Turkish Service, Andrew admits:

> Well, I didn't know that I was going to be released because I was
> actually declared guilty. . . . We spent our time, twenty-three years
> in Turkey, working in churches and telling people about Jesus Christ,
> showing his love to people. So we had nothing to do with any kind of
> terrorism. . . . In fact, we tried to bless Turkey, and we often prayed
> for Turkey. So it was a surprise when we were accused of terrorism.
> . . . But when I heard that they were convicting me, giving me a
> three-year sentence, and then releasing me because of time already
> served . . . then I was very relieved.[1]

Both Andrew and his wife Norine expressed gratitude. Norine said, "First, we thank God because he's the one that did it. And he did it through the prayers of . . . all the Christians from all kinds of different churches that for some reason this was in their heart to pray for us." Andrew added, "We believe God did it. But God uses people, and he also used people in setting us free."[2]

While Pastor Brunson's release was headline news, thousands of people are being released every single day without obvious fanfare. From prisons of shame, addiction, abuse, guilt, despair, regret—sometimes not even guilty of the circumstances that imprisoned them in the first place.

Jesus came to proclaim the release and freedom of captives and prisoners. This is good news for you and me. And we don't even need an earthly government official to intervene on our behalf! Jesus is our High Priest who "is able to save completely those who come to God through him, because he always lives to intercede for them" (Hebrews 7:25 NIV).

Are you enslaved to something or someone? Do you long to be released to live in freedom?

I once read about a man who noticed that huge circus elephants were roped to a tent pole with only a thin rope, one they surely could break in order to get free. When he asked the caretaker about this, he was told that when elephants were very young, they were trained by being roped to a tent pole with this same rope, which at that age they were unable to break for escape. As they grow up into adult elephants and greatly increase their strength, they do not realize that such a feeble rope cannot still hold them. So they remain tied and bound.

You are not who you used to be. It (whatever "it" is) is no longer strong enough to hold you back.

God is continually strengthening and sustaining you through each challenging life experience. Will you make a choice to be released?

Of course, it can be a long process. But it does begin with asking God to orchestrate your release. As Pastor Brunson says, "God uses people." Perhaps you could begin by seeking out spiritual or professional counseling or intervention. Do the hard work of confession, relinquishment, and restoration.

After Charles Wesley's own release from a life of legalism he penned these remarkable words: "My chains fell off, my heart was free; I rose, went forth and followed Thee. Amazing love, how can it be, that Thou, my God should die for me!" ("And Can It Be").

That sound you hear? Chains falling off . . .

Lord, I'm tired of being enslaved. But sometimes I'm even more fearful of what might be required of me with freedom. Thank You for not only bringing release but also guidance and empowerment for a whole new life. Amen.

How Will I Choose Release?

_____

_____

_____

_____

_____

_____

_____

_____

_____

_____

_____

_____

_____

_____

Choose Surrender

Father, if you are willing, please take this cup of suffering away from me. Yet I want your will to be done, not mine.

—Luke 22:42

Sitting on the floor of the attic after uncovering a little ceramic plaque, I realized anew how letting go must be one of the hardest choices a person ever has to make.

The plaque displayed a Dutch prayer, the English translation carefully handwritten on the back by a young Dutch mother who had made her home in the United States.

> Father, I lay the names of my children in Your hands.
> Engrave their names therein with permanent script.
> Allow nothing and no one ever to burn them out.
> Though Satan may seek to sift them as wheat.
> Hold fast to them when I must let go.
> And always let your power stand above their weakness.
> You know how merciless the world will hate them
> If they do not walk or follow in its way.
> I do not ask You to spare my children every sorrow,

> But be their comfort when they are lonely and afraid.
> For your name's sake keep them in your covenant.
> Let them never stray from You, never as long as life shall last!
> I lay the names of my children in Your hands. Amen.

I know from the inscribed date that shortly after translating this poem, Inka was diagnosed with cancer from which she soon died. She left behind her husband and three small children, the youngest only a year old.

Surrender indeed—wanting what God wants more than what we want.

> As long as you maintain your own personal interests and ambitions, you cannot be completely aligned or identified with God's interests. This can only be accomplished by giving up all of your personal plans once and for all, and by allowing God to take you directly into His purpose for the world. Your understanding of your ways must also be surrendered, because they are now the ways of the Lord. —Oswald Chambers, *My Utmost for His Highest*[1]

True surrender is freely choosing to let go—laying all in God's capable hands.

That's exactly what Abraham did when God asked him to sacrifice his only son Isaac on the altar. He surrendered to the one He knew and trusted.

Can you live today with that sort of abandoned trust in God?

Almost forty years ago that young Dutch mother opened her hands and laid her children in God's larger ones. The symbolic act became a literal one when she died too young from cancer. But God was faithful. One day he placed those same children into the hands of another young woman who had surrendered her long desire to be a mother. *Me.* Perhaps one of the greatest grace gifts I have ever received is the privilege of adopting Inka's children and raising them to adulthood where they continue to know God's great care and enjoy full lives of service and surrender.

Long ago when I was in my thirties and wondering if I would ever be a wife and mama, I realized that as an act of consecration, I needed to release my own "toys"—my vision of what I thought would make me happy. You can do the same today with this classic prayer:

Father, I want to know Thee, but my coward heart fears to give up its toys. I cannot part with them without inward bleeding . . . I come trembling, but I do come. Please root from my heart all those things which I have cherished so long and which have become a very part of my living self, so that Thou mayest enter and dwell there without a rival. . . . Then shall my heart have no need of the sun to shine in it, for Thyself wilt be the light of it . . . In Jesus' Name, Amen. —A. W. Tozer, *The Pursuit of God*[2]

Lord, opening my clenched fists is such a challenge—I want to hold tightly to what I have. And yet I know it is only through surrender—letting go—that I can receive all You desire to give me. Please help me learn how to both relinquish and receive. Amen.

How Will I Choose Surrender?

_____

_____

_____

_____

_____

_____

_____

_____

Day 18

Choose Prayer

I took my troubles to the LORD, I cried out to him, and he answered
my prayer.

—Psalm 120:1

My friend Janet was sharing lunch with a friend when that friend con-
fessed, "I'm just not good at prayer."

Janet smiled and said, "But you just ordered exactly what you wanted
from the menu. You know what you need—just mention that to your heavenly Father."

Prayer can literally be that simple. Communicating your needs.

And so, I do. I talk to my heavenly Father. About everything and everyone. It's a conversation. I speak, then I spend time in silence listening. Sometimes the Holy Spirit actually impresses upon me words (often Scripture) I
believe are straight from God.

More often than not I spend entire conversations sitting across from an
empty chair and pouring out my heart to the One next to me. These may not
even be entreaties but rather joyful praises or gratitude lists for all God is and
has provided. And occasionally I have lain in bed, my cheeks wet with tears,
my heart aching from brokenness. No words. Just groans. That's prayer too.

Most days my husband and I carve out a time to pray together—lifting up names of our loved ones, specific friends who are grieving or ill,

colleagues in ministry around the world, and the myriad concerns dominating the news. We always conclude by praying the Lord's Prayer together. And I make a point of thinking and speaking slowly each familiar word with intentionality, lest it become rote.

> Prayer is a simple confession of faith—that God exists and listens and answers. . . . Jesus reminds us through the Lord's Prayer that taking our needs to the Father is not a complicated affair. Our simple words with our simple humbled attitude are all we need to make the prayer perfect. —Janet Holm McHenry, *The Complete Guide to the Prayers of Jesus*[1]

For me, prayer is more of a way of life than something I do. It's part of who I am. The Apostle Paul admonished us to "Pray all the time" (1 Thessalonians 5:17 *The Message*). Sometimes that looks like verbal arrows I shoot up quickly in the midst of crisis ("Help!") or relief ("Thanks!"). Sometimes my prayers are through the words of a hymn I'm singing while driving or walking or washing dishes.

When my four children were young, I hugged and prayed over them before they caught the bus to school. Praying for their teacher by name was part of that ritual as well. Today those young adults are scattered around the world with children of their own. But when we wrap up a phone conversation, I often end it with a short prayer. I suppose they are used to that. I do the same thing with folks who contact me about speaking or writing—they may not be as used to finishing such an exploratory conversation in prayer. It's a great reminder to ask God to guide us all in this potential collaboration.

Today I was part of my weekly online Bible study with about ten other author/speakers from around the country. Our hour ended up being spent entirely with prayer requests and praying over one another. The assigned study could wait. Our many needs could not. We were simply there for one another, praying for miracles from the God of miracles. I can hardly wait to see what He will do.

Do you pray boldly?

Don't you know *God is for you*? One pastor says this is an indicator of a healthy prayer life.

> If you don't believe [God is for you], then you'll pray small timid prayers; if you do believe it, then you'll pray big audacious prayers. And one way or another, your small timid prayers or big audacious prayers will change the trajectory of your life . . . *who you become* is determined by *how you pray.* —Mark Batterson, *The Circle Maker: Praying Circles Around Your Biggest Dreams and Greatest Fears*[2]

Will you choose to become a strong woman of prayer? God always answers. *Yes. No. Wait.* We love some answers and struggle with others. And His timeline is often different from ours. Sometimes He withholds, knowing there is something even better in store. But this is who He is. Faithful. A promise keeper. Remember, "If you have the faith to dream big, pray hard, and think long, there is nothing God loves more than proving His faithfulness."[3]

Lord, may I never take this communication with You for granted. What a privilege to pour out my heart in prayer—both the petitions and the praises. You are as close as my very breath—may Your name forever be on my lips. Amen.

How Will I Choose Prayer?

_____

_____

_____

_____

_____

_____

_____

Day 19

Choose Strength

He gives power to the weak and strength to the powerless.

—Isaiah 40:29

*O*nce as strong as his childhood friend, Justin Skeesuck soon found himself confined to a wheelchair, unable to walk or care for all his needs.

Diagnosed with Multifocal acquired motor axonopathy, a neuromuscular disease similar to ALS, Justin was determined to do something everyone said he could never do—complete the Camino de Santiago trail. This journey—a spiritual pilgrimage since the ninth century to the believed burial site of the Apostle James—winds through five hundred miles of mountains, forests, and fields in northern Spain.

When he shared with his friend Patrick Gray that the Camino was "calling him," Justin heard these words from his best friend—"I'll push you."

However, neither man realized how physically and emotionally taxing the trip would be. Not only did they have a strict time limit—about six weeks to get from start to finish—but they also faced incredibly challenging obstacles. With Patrick Gray pushing Justin Skeesuck in a three-wheeled aluminum wheelchair, the pair traversed the mountain ranges, crossed rivers, and navigated a desert.[1]

Throughout the numerous mental and physical challenges, time and time again their strength was an echo of what the Apostle Paul declared, "For when I am weak, then I am strong" (2 Corinthians 12:10).

As followers of Christ, both men took away valuable lessons from this journey.

For Gray, it forced him to see that the person he was and the person he hoped to be weren't the same, and that he'd given his family reason to question how much he valued them. . . . For Skeesuck, he said, it restored his faith in humanity. "My realization after coming through this pilgrimage and meeting the people we've met beyond our journey is that there are so many good people in this world doing amazing things and good things. I'm so blessed to witness it—to be at the front end of the roller coaster and to have people step in and help me."[2]

Where do you feel weak in your own life? Where has pain drained you of all physical, emotional, and perhaps even spiritual strength? If you spend your life clinging to the idea that this never should have happened—*it isn't fair*—then you may just miss the power that could be yours.

One Christian psychologist is quick to say this choice—to call upon an inner resource you may not even know you have—will actually determine your destiny. Will your pain and weakness make you bitter or better?

Your healing hangs on the hinge of this life-changing choice. It's the choice to surrender your desire to have life go the way you planned it. Simply put, it is the choice to find strength in your struggle. It is the choice to find hope in your hurt. It is the choice to choose the direction of your life and the demeanor of your spirit. In short, it is the determination to make the best of the worst. —Les Parrott, *You're Stronger Than You Think: The Power to Do What You Feel You Can't*[3]

Will you choose God's strength when you find yourself at your weakest point? "Those who trust in the LORD will find new strength" (Isaiah 40:31).

If you need fresh strength, will you trust God in the dangerous, in the risky, in what seems to be impossible?

It is no accident that I happened to watch the documentary film, *I'll Push You,* about Justin and Patrick's journey on the night before our family embarked on a frightening health adventure. Just remembering their courage and perseverance helped me make some wise choices to discover I was stronger than I thought.

Through Jesus.

> *Lord, I feel like such a weakling most of the time—exhausted long before the day or the duties give out. Thank You for constant reminders that You are my strength, even (perhaps especially) when I feel I have none at all. Help me do the impossible, through You. Amen.*

How Will I Choose Strength?

_____

_____

_____

_____

_____

_____

_____

_____

_____

_____

_____

Choose Love

Don't just pretend to love others. Really love them. Hate what is wrong. Hold tightly to what is good. Love each other with genuine affection, and take delight in honoring each other.

—Romans 12:9–10

Love *is.* And love *does.*

My home church's motto is "Love God and Love Others."

The Beatles sang, "All you need is love."

"Love Is a Battlefield" was a 1980s pop song that sold a million copies.

"I Love NY" is a popular state slogan.

One restaurant calls itself "We Love Burgers."

These random examples clearly make the case for why we are so confused about love. When we use the word for *everything* from loving our husband to loving hamburgers, the word is in danger of losing value.

But one truth I discovered a long time ago: *I cannot love others until I first receive the unconditional love of God for myself.* My Creator declares "I have loved you with an everlasting love; I have drawn you with unfailing kindness" (Jeremiah 31:3 NIV).

Do you believe God loves you unconditionally?

The word used in Jeremiah 31:3 for *love* is translated from the original Hebrew word *chesed* and is often translated "everlasting love" or "unfailing kindness." Both are parts of this large word. Bible scholar Eugene Peterson says, "No single word in our language is adequate to translate it, so we revert to the use of adjectives to bring out the distinctive quality and broad reach of this love."[1]

Yes, we first receive such love from God, but then we are called to generously dole out love as well. Peterson continues, "We humans, who have been created in the image of God, are also capable of loving this way, even though we never seem to get very good at it. *Chesed* is love without regard to shifting circumstances, hormones, emotional states, and personal convenience."[2]

I recently taught a summer midweek Bible study—a time when most New Englanders are "at the shore." I decided to call it "Finding Answers Together" and tackle some of today's pressing dilemmas. Needless to say, on the week scheduled for answers to the question, "How do I love difficult, different, and demanding people?" the room was packed. Some people even came home from the shore to be there!

Because, how *do* we make the choice to love someone who appears unlovable?

Shannan Martin and her family discovered the answer by radically changing their lifestyle, moving into the inner city, and intentionally noticing others around them.

> In our heads, we understand that everything we accomplish is pointless if we cannot be known as people who love freely and fully. . . . As our love for our place deepens, our love for its people will flourish. . . . This is how we love, by focusing so intently on each other that we can't help ourselves. We watch from our windows. We venture outside. We receive the help that's offered. We find ourselves connected in spite of everything we once thought stood between us. . . . We taste the possibility and power of ordinary, luminous love, and discover we can't get enough. —Shannan Martin, *The Ministry of Ordinary Places: Waking Up to God's Goodness Around You*[3]

The Martins embody today's verse, "Don't just pretend to love others. Really love them," which is practically impossible unless we learn to look at others with fresh eyes.

International attorney Bob Goff does this by first admitting the people we often see as a problem, God sees as sons and daughters made in His image. He offers challenging yet promising words when he says, "Who has been mean or rude or flat wrong or creeps you out? Don't tell them all your opinions; give them all your love. I know it's hard for you. It's hard for me too. . . . You'll also be misunderstood—you might not even understand yourself anymore. . . . As you practice loving everybody, always, what will happen along the way is, you'll no longer be who you used to be. God will turn you into love."[4]

May God turn us into love today. And may that love be part of healing our fragmented world.

Lord, I realize it's the most important commandment and yet the hardest to perfect—love. Please help me discover new ways to always make it a verb in my own life—a choice toward those who need love the most. You know who they are; show me. Amen

How Will I Choose Love?

_____

_____

_____

_____

_____

_____

_____

_____

_____

Choose Patience

We also pray that you will be strengthened with all his glorious power so you will have all the endurance and patience you need. May you be filled with joy.

—Colossians 1:11

I did not interrupt. I restrained myself from finishing his sentence or, worse, saying something catty like "hanging by a thread here."

Instead, I patiently waited. For his brain to finally download the correct words and for his mouth to process them. It was excruciatingly tedious. For me. But, oh, so much more so for him.

For nearly two years my husband Mike experienced mobility challenges—an involuntary weaving while trying to navigate something as simple as the sidewalk in our neighborhood. Eventually he hesitated to venture out very far, concerned he might not make his destination. At the same time, he couldn't problem solve the most ordinary of tasks such as sending an email—this cognitive memory loss was both frustrating and frightening. Everything seemed to take so much time. We sought many doctors and medical tests, but his problems remained undiagnosed and were getting worse.

One of the best things I could do for Mike was to choose patience. Always.

For some of you, this may sound like a breeze; others will identify with someone like me for whom patience has been a lifelong struggle. I remember as a young woman praying for this particular aspect of the fruit of the Spirit—"Lord, give me patience, and give it to me *now!*"

The more I longed for patience, the more agitated I became. Is it any surprise impatience causes negative emotions? Frustration, irritation, and anger can elevate our stress levels, which impacts our overall health. Chronic impatience throws life into imbalance both physically and spiritually. And even when the current challenge is resolved (Mike's illness was eventually diagnosed and treated) we must still pursue this valuable quality of the fruit of the Spirit.

Patience is a byproduct of a soul at peace, a person who cares more for others—especially those who are slow because they are struggling. Oh, I could have counted to ten (or twenty). I could have willed myself to be patient as Mike searched for the right words to communicate. But how much better to actually *become* a person of serenity for whom patience is the fruit?

When Paul lists the qualities of love in 1 Corinthians 13, patience comes first: "Love is patient and kind" (v. 4). The conclusion would be that my love for my husband is made evident through my patience with him. Healthy human relationships are built on the foundation of patience. Later, in his letter to the Ephesians, Paul goes on to say, "Always be humble and gentle. Be patient with each other, making allowance for each other's faults because of your love. Make every effort to keep yourselves united in the Spirit, binding yourselves together with peace" (Ephesians 4:2–3).

How can you be more patient?

Slow down. Impatience comes from thinking you need to hurry.

Breathe deeply, and will yourself to relax in the situation.

Put yourself in another's shoes, and treat them as you would want to be treated.

Give up your need to be right or in control.

Ask God to help you understand and value that person's worth.

Silently pray a short prayer for God's help and presence.

> The more we love others, the easier it is to be patient with them. . . . Patience comes when we let go of ourselves, our desires, our agenda, our goals, our control. . . . Patience requires us to pay attention, to focus on something besides ourselves. Patience is when we value others ahead of ourselves. —Tyler Edwards, "Christians Need to Recover the Lost Art of Patience"[1]

As we seek to always view others as worthy and made in God's image, we will discover that patience flows freely. It is not an option for Christ-followers, but one more way in which we can extend love and mercy to others.

Lord, first of all I want to thank You for small victories I am making in an effort to be more patient. Help me continue to look out for others and to resist hurry. May I also discover much joy along the slow(er) path. Amen.

How Will I Choose Patience?

_____

_____

_____

_____

_____

_____

_____

_____

Day 22

Choose to Sing

The LORD is my strength and shield. I trust him with all my heart. He helps me, and my heart is filled with joy. I burst out in songs of thanksgiving.

—Psalm 28:7

With a terrible voice and an impossible dream, Florence Foster Jenkins achieved her impossible when she sang to a sold-out crowd at Carnegie Hall in 1944. Reportedly, one month later and before her death, she said, "People may say I *couldn't* sing, but no one can ever say I *didn't* sing."

Do you sing? If not, what is your excuse? Bad voice? Nothing to sing about?

Paul and Silas chose to sing while chained in the dark, dank dungeon of a Roman prison. They had been stripped and beaten, yet even in the midst of such torture, they drew out of the depths of their being musical praise to the God who was with them in the hardest of places. God gave them "songs in the night" (Job 35:10) that were used to change heaven and earth as God sent an earthquake to free them and draw both prisoners and warden to the Source of all music. (See Acts 16.)

In the midst of another dark time—the Civil War—Robert Lowry wrote a hymn reminding us to make the same choice:

What though my joys and comforts die?
The Lord my Savior liveth.
What though the darkness gather round?
Songs in the night He giveth.
No storm can shake my inmost calm,
While to that Rock I'm clinging;
Since Christ is Lord of heaven and earth,
How can I keep from singing?

—Robert Lowry, "How Can I Keep from Singing?"

Someone once said, "She who sings prays twice."

How incredible that we have been given such a way to communicate with our Creator, Redeemer, and Sustainer! Songwriters Keith and Kristyn Getty say, "We sing knowing that our Lord's ears are open and listening as we lift our voices to Him with intelligent, sincere, and joy-filled words and notes. . . . The songs we sing to ourselves are what tether us to our Lord day by day. The songs we sing to others are what proclaim His kingdom manifesto in a way that reaches deep into their heads and their hearts."[1]

The entire Book of Psalms is a songbook, and God's people have been singing throughout time and eternity. "Worship the LORD with gladness. Come before him, singing with joy" (Psalm 100:2). We are called to both sing and serve. So I sing. Often. Alone and, yes, even when others can hear me. Believe me, those songs come from deep within my soul, and like in today's text, I "burst out in songs."

Those very songs are full of strength. When pastor Mark Batterson reflected on Psalm 32:7 (NIV), "You will protect me from trouble and surround me with songs of deliverance," he said, "Did you know that God is singing songs of deliverance all around you all the time? . . . Those songs of deliverance are powerful enough to break any bondage, overcome any addiction, and solve any problem."[2]

I have discovered that singing can change a whole atmosphere. Singing along to the standards of Frank Sinatra and Judy Garland while I'm cleaning the house reminds me of my childhood and brings great memories of my parents. Singing along with praise music or hymns in the midst of a funk raises my spirits. Singing aloud to and with my grandchildren makes us all feel joyful and connected. And yes, I close every single speaking presentation by singing/praying over my audience.

As long as I am able "I will sing about your power. Each morning I will sing with joy about your unfailing love" (Psalm 59:16).

> So sing! The song of rejoicing softens hard hearts. It makes tears of godly sorrow flow from them. Singing summons the Holy Spirit. Happy praises offered in simplicity and love lead the faithful to complete harmony without discord. Don't stop singing. —Hildegard of Bingen[3]

Lord, You have given me a voice—one to use, no matter the musical quality. May the sounds that come forth always be pleasing to You, while at the same time directing others to the great Source of all beauty and music. Truly it is a healing power. Amen.

How Will I Choose to Sing?

_____

_____

_____

_____

_____

_____

_____

DAY 23

Choose With

The virgin will conceive a child! She will give birth to a son and will call him Immanuel (which means "God is with us").

—Isaiah 7:14

"ow many moments of my life today can I fill with a conscious awareness of and surrender to God's presence?" author John Ortberg asked himself. He wanted so much to embrace what he called the "with God" life.

But after rushing halfway through the day without even thinking about God, he could almost hear Him speaking, and he recorded those thoughts, as though God were speaking directly to him, in his book:

John, let's look at the next two hours. You will go through those two hours of your life with me or without me. You can continue doing life without me and feel stressed, pressured, angry, sorry for yourself, impatient, and be a pain in the neck to the people around you. Or you can do those two hours with me. . . . You can be grateful you were given a life. You can be joyful when you actually have work to do, and you can recognize that I, not you, am running the universe. . . . What's it going to be, John?

Needless to say, John Ortberg answered his own inner discussion with, "Yes, God. I want to do life with you. My soul needs you more than it needs my frustration and impatience."[1]

I confess that all too often I have not chosen the "with God" life but have simply run around doing my own thing, with the occasional arrow prayer shot up to the heavens out of need. How much richer it would be to intentionally acknowledge Him beside me each step of the way by breathing deeply and invoking the peace He grants, praying softly as unexpected news arrives, and summoning strength and courage through a recitation of scriptural promises. Each act an offering up—confirming not only is Christ *with me*, but I have also chosen to be *with Him*.

The incarnation of Jesus was God's way of bringing us together. To abide. He didn't just *yell down* from on high, cheering us on life's journey. He *came down*. "God with us." So that we would never be alone.

God with us. That is what separates Christianity from every other religion. What other deity would stoop to enter our world?

> [God's] plan to restore his creation was not to send a list of rules and rituals to follow, nor was it the implementation of useful principles. He did not send a genie to grant us our desires, nor did he give us a task to accomplish. Instead God himself came to be with us—to walk with us once again as he had done in Eden in the beginning. Jesus entered into our dark existence to share our broken world and to illuminate a different way forward. —Skye Jethani, *With: Reimagining the Way You Relate to God*[2]

Are you living "with God" every moment of every day?

Each day gifts us with 86,400 seconds. Why not try to intentionally live each of these moments with God? Just begin. Invite God in as you awaken, and thank Him for His presence as you lay your head on the pillow.

And in-between, try to see others with the eyes of God. When you approach the cashier at the coffee bar, behave as though both you and Jesus-beside-you were placing an order. How would He do it? What might He say? Remember, "From now on we regard no one from a worldly point of view" (2 Corinthians 5:16 NIV).

How can the word *with* change your own perspective of journeying through life? And how will you pass this goodness along to others?

Perhaps this vignette from the life of Billy Graham might encourage that sense of God's continual presence. One day in 1982 the staff at *Today* was expecting the famous evangelist for a special appearance. In their efforts to accommodate Mr. Graham, the producer's assistant informed the Graham team that a private room was available for Mr. Graham to pray in before the broadcast. Declining the offer, Mr. Graham's team member gently explained to the somewhat shocked assistant, "Mr. Graham started praying when he got up this morning, he prayed while he was eating breakfast, he prayed on the way over here in the car they sent for us, and he'll probably be praying all through the interview."[3]

No special set-up room was necessary because Mr. Graham knew he was "with" God anywhere and everywhere already. On one level engaging in the people and activities of his day while on a deeper level in constant communion with God.

May we do the same.

> *Lord, one of the great mysteries of life is that You would humble Yourself and become one of us. But because You did, I know beyond a shadow of a doubt that You are constantly with me. May I always, always choose to walk with You. Amen.*

How Will I Choose With?

_____

_____

_____

_____

_____

_____

_____

_____

_____

_____

_____

_____

_____

_____

_____

_____

_____

_____

_____

_____

_____

_____

_____

Choose Less

And why worry about your clothing? Look at the lilies of the field and how they grow. They don't work or make their clothing, yet Solomon in all his glory was not dressed as beautifully as they are. And if God cares so wonderfully for wildflowers that are here today and thrown into the fire tomorrow, he will certainly care for you.

—Matthew 6:28–30

To be honest, it's not only time—it's *past* time.

To clean my closet. Actually, to purge my closet. It's not a walk-in but rather a 1940s cubicle built when wardrobes were simpler. And less. Perhaps a better way to live.

I have done this before. Seasonally. Well, at least once a year. But sadly, no matter how many black garbage bags are hauled out for trash or donation, the remaining garments always seem to multiply.

"Hello, my name is Lucinda. And I have too many clothes—way too many." In my defense, they cover a range of sizes and seasons, options and occasions. Just in case.

But that day rarely comes. And honey, I've got better things to do than spend time trying to decide what to wear!

Recently I learned a new (to me) term: capsule wardrobe, which is a small wardrobe made up of versatile pieces you love to wear. Each season you clear your closet except for a set number of pieces, such as thirty-seven. Doing this clears up more time, money, and energy for things that really matter.

Could I make this daring choice? Could you?

Here's a plan to help you get started:

Pick a day off and forbid anyone else from entering the bedroom all day.

Purchase a box of large black garbage bags.

Empty your entire closet on the bed (this will ensure you finish by bedtime).

Move each item into one of these piles:

Keep: because you love it or it's a staple

Maybe: saving for its proper season or can't decide yet (limit to one bag)

Donate: so someone else can enjoy

Trash: if beyond repair or need

Review your Keep pile. How many items do you have? If more than thirty-seven (or whatever number you chose), move more clothes into the Maybe, Donate, or Trash piles.

When the final step came—putting it all back into the tiny closet—I was amazed. And a bit anxious. *Can I really make this work?*

I want to make this work.

Minimalist Courtney has been choosing less for eight years and lists many benefits of a capsule wardrobe:

1.) I need way less than I think to be happy. 2.) No one cares what I'm wearing. 3.) Deciding what to wear requires mental energy better spent on other things. 4.) A simple closet is the gateway to a simple life. 5.) Simplicity is the way back to love. . . . Imagine what would happen if you invested most of the time, money, and energy you spend on your clothes on the person underneath them. —Courtney Carver, *Soulful Simplicity: How Living with Less Can Lead to So Much More*[1]

I'm on my way. Will you join me?

> *Lord, I have way more stuff than I need. I confess I have given in to wanting more, just to satisfy something deep inside. Will You fill those empty spaces and give me joy in reducing my lifestyle of consumption? Amen.*

How Will I Choose Less?

_____

_____

_____

_____

_____

_____

_____

_____

_____

_____

_____

_____

_____

_____

_____

_____

_____

DAY 25

Choose Serenity

But blessed is the man who trusts me, GOD, the woman who sticks with GOD. They're like trees replanted in Eden, putting down roots near the rivers—never a worry through the hottest of summers, never dropping a leaf, serene and calm through droughts, bearing fresh fruit every season.

—Jeremiah 17:7–8 *The Message*

*E*nough already! One final interruption to my well-made plans had pushed me off the edge into the black hole of chaos, confusion, and helplessness. I was undone. Exhausted. Overwhelmed. Worst of all, everything happening *inside* was spilling *outside* over everyone else. It wasn't pretty.

I longed to be a woman who exuded peacefulness and calm. The Amplified Bible, Classic Edition expands on such serenity: "So, beloved, since you are expecting these things, be eager to be found by Him [at His coming] without spot or blemish and at peace [in serene confidence, free from fears and agitating passions and moral conflicts]" (2 Peter 3:14).

A lifetime of following Jesus has taught me that a woman of serenity is:

Still

One who takes time to "be still, and know that [he is] God" (Psalm 46:10) realizes many problems can be solved simply by slowing down and seeking silence. Hurry is the great enemy of soul care, so she deliberately takes precious time to be still.

Established

One who knows her primary identity is not based on her roles in life or specific hats she wears (which can change often) but on the fact she is God's beloved. Known. Seen. Called. This gives her a confidence, which is beautiful.

Restored

One who has walked through challenge and suffering and has emerged on the other side renewed and refreshed. She has worked through the healing process and allowed God to repurpose her pain and restore her worth.

Empowered

One who knows ultimate power is from God through the Holy Spirit. While she deliberately seeks a healthy physical life, she also knows inner strength comes through daily disciplines and spiritual practices.

Nurtured

One who places a priority on that which nurtures her creativity and her soul, like long walks through the countryside, a cup of hot tea on fine bone china, reading a book that challenges both her mind and spirit, celebrating cozy moments with dear friends, enjoying music and laughter.

Inspired

One who continually consults God's Word for wisdom and guidance each day. She finds inspiration through stories of the saints and sinners who held on to faith. She discovers courage to radically reach out to serve a hurting world in Jesus' name.

Thankful

One who knows the Source of all gifts and turns to God in daily gratitude. She makes note of His many blessings because, "Who can list the glorious miracles of the LORD? Who can ever praise Him enough?" (Psalm 106:2).

Yielding

One who is willing to surrender all her plans and purposes into the hands of a sovereign God learns to hold everything loosely as God gives and takes away. She is resilient and steadfast amidst the many changing fortunes of life.

Will you make the choices that lead to serenity?

Lord, sometimes these qualities of serenity baffle me. And yet, as I read them, one-by-one I realize that with Your help, they are truly attainable. May I seek the life that exudes calm, peace, and spiritual confidence so others may be strengthened and drawn to You. Amen.

How Will I Choose Serenity?

_____

_____

_____

_____

_____

_____

_____

_____

_____

Choose Nurture

God's various gifts are handed out everywhere; but they all origi-
nate in God's Spirit. . . . Each person is given something to do that
shows who God is: Everyone gets in on it, everyone benefits. All
kinds of things are handed out by the Spirit, and to all kinds of
people!

—1 Corinthians 12:4–7 *The Message*

What would you like to be when you grow up?" I asked my then three-
year-old one day.

Maggie put down her microphone (a wooden spoon) and stepped away
from the her stage (the fireplace hearth) and quickly replied, "A star!"

She had been entertaining me with her own rendition of Aretha
Franklin's "R-E-S-P-E-C-T" (as only a baby-boomer mama could enjoy), so I
shouldn't have been too surprised at her answer. Already she was a singing/
dancing/acting ball of energy, and that was long before I had even heard of
the term "triple threat" or "musical theatre degree."

I suspect few Christian parents pray fervently that their children will end
up in the world of entertainment. Then again, God is the One who made our
daughter and bestowed upon her unique gifts and talents—"something to
do that shows who God is."

My most important job as a mama? To nurture each unique child and help them grow into the person God created them to be.

Not to make them who *I* want them to be. And not to try and live my life through theirs.

Are you doing all you can to nurture growth and fulfillment in your children? The whole process begins by listening and observing—discovering their strengths and weaknesses and the way God has uniquely orchestrated their minds, emotions, bodies, and hearts. This takes an investment of time and energy. We cannot simply be drive-by parents waving and shouting an occasional "Way to go, girl!" or "Look out for that bump ahead, buddy!"

And chances are, if you're a parent, each of your children will be different from the other. As soon as you have the oldest figured out, you must start from scratch with the next one. But this is also the joy of being a mama. I firmly believe whoever said "variety is the spice of life" was most certainly talking about my two sons and two daughters.

My eldest son, born with special needs, is much like me—blossoming from words of encouragement and affirmation. He's an overcomer, friendly, and brave, and has now lived in his own apartment and worked at the same restaurant for more than twenty years. My second son always loved the outdoors and extreme sports. This former Eagle Scout now enjoys hard work, fly fishing, skiing dropped from a helicopter, mountain biking, and hunting all the meat he eats. It's no surprise he lives in Montana and competes in CrossFit!

My first daughter was born brilliant and destined to help change the world through compassionate international development. Yes, I worried whenever she took off for overseas assignments in dangerous places, but it was always to set up programs for marginalized women and children. Now she lives across the pond and juggles her work with motherhood.

And that little girl singing into the wooden spoon? We established boundaries and did our best to instill godly values in her and her siblings. But we also encouraged opportunity and risk. Today she is a professional actress performing on Broadway and balancing a full life of family, friends, and faith. Most certainly a star in my book.

Will you choose to nurture your own child to live their unique life story?

I've discovered this works best when we mamas have already figured out who God called *us* to be—when we exemplify values and vocation with passion and purpose. When we trust God so much we can choose to *entrust* our most precious ones to His plan.

> *Lord, the children You have placed in my life are such a blessing— and sometimes a puzzle! Please show me who You have created them to become and then guide and empower me to best urge them to live that unique story. Amen.*

How Will I Choose Nurture?

_____

_____

_____

_____

_____

_____

_____

_____

_____

_____

_____

_____

_____

Day 27

Choose Covenant

The LORD is the witness between you and the wife of your youth. . . .
She is your partner, the wife of your marriage covenant.

—Malachi 2:14 NIV

All around the church they began standing up. Some struggled and were gently supported by their spouse with a hand or cane or even wheelchair. But everyone seemed happy to be recognized. And honored.

That Sunday our church was celebrating all the couples who had been married more than fifty years. And there were twenty-six couples! That's a minimum of 1,300 years of marriage, but of course quite a few had been married for more than fifty. In fact, I spent most of the reception talking with my neighbors who were celebrating seventy-two years of marriage that year.

There was a wedding cake. And punch and coffee. But mostly there was joy. Gratitude for the faithfulness of God and the perseverance of the men and women who had chosen to honor their vows said so very long ago.

Since Mike and I were both in our thirties when we said our own marriage vows thirty-five years ago, I've often wondered if we would make it to our own golden anniversary.

I cringe when I remember that long-ago day when Mike took off his wedding ring and put it on the table beside me.

I was crushed. He had every right to be frustrated, even angry, in the middle of our disagreement. I'm stubborn and intense and have a way of pushing too hard. But he did eventually put his ring back on, and we have continued to make every effort to keep our covenant, by God's grace.

Sadly, many people today look at marriage as more of a contract ("I will love you as long as you fulfill the need I have right now, but when you can't, I'm gone") than a covenant ("My love for you is a binding relationship of love and commitment that takes precedence over my changing needs and desires"). It usually takes a lifetime to experience that deep kind of loving, which is rarely the same as we felt on our wedding day. Covenant love is what shows up in those inevitable times when our spouse disappoints or rejects us.

And it all comes down to making a choice. Daily.

What do we do on those days when feelings of affection and delight cannot be sustained? Pastor Timothy Keller and his wife Kathy suggest this choice:

> When that happens you must remember that the essence of a marriage is that it is a covenant, a commitment, a promise of future love. So what do you do? You *do* the acts of love, despite your lack of feeling. You may not feel tender, sympathetic, and eager to please, but in your actions, you must *be* tender, understanding, forgiving, and helpful. . . . This is what can happen if you decide to love. —*The Meaning of Marriage: Facing the Complexities of Commitment and the Wisdom of God*[1]

God makes a covenant with us, and we in turn make covenants with one another. As Mike and my wedding Scripture clearly states, "They will be my people, and I will be their God. . . . I will make an everlasting covenant with them: I will never stop doing good for them. . . . I will find joy doing good for them and will faithfully and wholeheartedly replant them in this land" (Jeremiah 32:38–41).

Perhaps you are one of those who wanted desperately to keep your own marriage vows, but for a variety of reasons that covenant was broken. Be assured that though you are no longer married, the covenant between you and God can stay strong for the rest of your life.

In the Book of Hosea, God tells His wandering chosen people that He is making a covenant with them: "I will make you my wife forever, showing you righteousness and justice, unfailing love and compassion. I will be faithful to you and make you mine, and you will finally know me as the LORD" (Hosea 2:19–20).

Today will you choose to live your covenant with God and, if married, with your spouse?

> *Lord, I must admit that the promise of covenant sounds great when I am on the receiving end. But when it means I have to give—or worse, give up—then the struggle comes. Please help me to make the choice to keep all my promises—to You and my spouse. Amen.*

How Will I Choose Covenant?

_____

_____

_____

_____

_____

_____

_____

_____

_____

_____

_____

Choose Joy

Dear brothers and sisters, when troubles of any kind come your way, consider it an opportunity for great joy.

—James 1:2

Joy, which was the small publicity of the pagan, is the gigantic secret of the Christian. —G. K. Chesterton, *Orthodoxy*

What is the difference between joy and happiness? As best I can figure, happiness is dependent upon circumstances—our emotional response to experiencing something good. Joy, on the other hand, is a *choice we make*, regardless of circumstances.

Joy is the attitude that no matter what is going on around us, we can be peaceful inside by connecting with the bigger picture of God's great love.

One friend puts it this way, "It isn't fake happiness; it's bolder and more daring. It's staring right into the face of hardship and saying *my God is still good* and anchoring your heart in that truth. It's being thankful there is always joy to be chosen, thankfulness to be spoken, and that God's goodness cannot be broken."

How can you dare to choose joy today no matter what is going on around you?

Eugene Peterson believes joy has a history. When we choose to remember some of the great things God has done for us, we are filled yet again with joy. Our joy is nurtured by knowing what was characteristic of God's provision in our past is also available to us today and into our future. Why would God suddenly stop being present and powerful with us?

> This joy is not dependent on our good luck in escaping hardship. It is not dependent on our good health and avoidance of pain. Christian joy is actual in the midst of pain, suffering, loneliness and misfortune. —Eugene Peterson, *A Long Obedience in the Same Direction: Discipleship in an Instant Society*[1]

Scripture constantly lifts up our need for joy. "I pray that God, the source of hope, will fill you completely with joy and peace because you trust in him. Then you will overflow with confident hope through the power of the Holy Spirit" (Romans 15:13).

> [Jesus] prayed that you would have the same joy that the Father had given Him: a divine joy, a joy that comes from a deep and unwavering relationship with the Father. It is a joy that is grounded so firmly in a relationship with God that no change in circumstances could ever shake it. —Henry Blackaby and Richard Blackaby, *Experiencing God Day by Day*[2]

But how can we choose joy when life turned out so differently from the way we had hoped?

It is in those very places the enemy of our soul seeks to steal our joy. Bitterness, anger, brokenness, and frustration can become strongholds that give him access to our heart. Dwelling on the "if onlys" and "shoulds" cloud our perspective as they take root. That's why we choose instead to focus elsewhere: "Those who look to him for help will be radiant with joy; no shadow of shame will darken their faces" (Psalm 34:5).

My earliest memories of choosing joy date back to when I was about six years old and I adamantly informed Mama I did not want a doll for Christmas. But when Christmas came and there was no doll, I was despondent.

Exhibiting grace, she then took me all over our small town looking for a left-over doll—and I went home with a red-head, hard plastic-jointed one that every other holiday shopper had rejected. Somehow, this doll was perfect for me at that time. I named her Joy. I think now I chose that name so long ago because that's what *I* was seeking. Joy, the doll, still lives in my home.

Today, will you seek balance in your own life—the *joy* that is often accompanied by a struggle or sorrow?

> With every breath, how can you choose joy? It is a conscious, daily effort that can transform your life if you allow it to. Joy is a choice to see Him in the midst of daily moments, to call upon His Spirit's presence and strength at each turn, each curve in the road. Joy comes from being assured we are not alone in the dark places and that He is light and will shine His light in each place. —Sally Clarkson, "Learning How to Choose Joy"[3]

Lord, I'm a great one for fluctuating emotions based on circumstances. Happy when things go well, sad when they don't. What I really want more of is that permanent joy that sticks around no matter what is happening or not happening. Thank You for that. Amen.

How Will I Choose Joy?

_____

_____

_____

_____

_____

_____

_____

_____

_____

_____

_____

_____

_____

_____

_____

_____

_____

_____

_____

_____

_____

DAY 29

Choose Identity

It's in Christ that we find out who we are and what we are living for.
Long before we first heard of Christ and got our hopes up, he had
his eye on us, had designs on us for glorious living, part of the overall purpose he is working out in everything and everyone.

—Ephesians 1:11–12 *The Message*

*I*n the film *Simon Birch* based on John Irving's novel *A Prayer for Owen
Meany*, Simon and his best friend Joe are misfit boys living in Maine.
Simon was born with a type of dwarfism (Morquio's syndrome), and Joe
was born illegitimate. They often practice holding their breath underwater
for a very long time at the local swimming hole and eventually become
very good at this skill. Always convinced he was born for a noble purpose,
Simon perseveres throughout life, even when one of his actions inadvertently causes the death of someone he loves.

While viewing this film, one can't help but think Simon's confidence
is merely a crutch to help him get through life. But in reality, something
extraordinary happens that calls for a tiny person who can hold his breath
underwater a long time. When that need arises, Simon is enlisted, equipped,
and empowered to live out his unique identity with courage, faithfulness,
and the ultimate sacrifice.

Years later, his friend Joe—now grown up with his own son Simon in tow—kneels at Simon Birch's grave and reflects on how knowing him changed the course of his life—for good.

Where do you find your identity? Do you have a grasp on how God created you uniquely and what He requires of you in using the gifts and opportunities sent your way?

Discovering the answers to these questions and making choices to pursue them will possibly change the course of your own life.

As a young woman I wrestled with aspects of my identity due to rejection or praise from other people—how they viewed me threaded its way into how I viewed myself. Because, for better or for worse, identity is partly *bestowed* by others.

> We are who we are in relation to others. But far more important, we draw our identity from our impact on those others—*if* and *how* we affect them. We long to know that we make a difference in the lives of others, to know that we matter, that our presence cannot be replaced . . . [But then] we think we have to keep doing something in order to be desirable. Once we find something that will bring us some attention, we have to keep it going or risk the loss of the attention. —John Eldredge, *The Sacred Romance: Drawing Closer to the Heart of God*[1]

Eventually I jumped off this treadmill of attention seeking, at least for the most part. And you must do the same. "Once you had no identity as a people; now you are God's people. Once you received no mercy; now you have received God's mercy" (1 Peter 2:10).

Like many, I spent early years trying on different hats, desperately seeking a good fit. Was I cut out to be a social worker or a theologian? Would I write the great American novel or belt out country music songs from a stage? Though aware of certain gifts and talents, I was deplorably ignorant of some of my tendencies and traits. Basically, I had to try and risk, fail and attempt something else. I discovered that as I grew in my own faith journey, my identity began to emerge on its own.

And it had absolutely nothing to do with a job or title—my core identity became "beloved of God." I am loved by God.

> Identity is something that our Creator alone can bestow on us. As we journey through this life, we may catch glimpses of who we are—sinner, servant, manager, or consumer—but these are only broken images in a dim mirror. Our true selves . . . will only be revealed when we are fully *with* God. —Skye Jethani, *With: Reimagining the Way You Relate to God*[2]

I discovered myself in who God was in relation to me—*Abba* who loves His daughter.

One day the core of who you are will encounter a situation not unlike Simon Birch—one that calls for all God has fashioned you for such a time. When that happens, be you. For truly, as our passage from today says, it is "in Christ that we find out who we are and what we are living for."

> *You, and only you, can express a particular and specific aspect of God's character in this world of ours, and . . . what God is calling out of you is you!*[3]

> *Lord, I wonder why we spend so much time and energy trying to fit in when You created us to be distinct and different? Will You help me first of all to discover that special uniqueness You have called out in me, and then to live it to the fullest? Amen.*

How Will I Choose Identity?

_____

_____

_____

_____

_____

_____

_____

_____

_____

_____

_____

_____

_____

_____

_____

_____

_____

_____

_____

_____

_____

_____

_____

Day 30

Choose Forgiveness

> LORD, if you kept a record of our sins, who, O LORD, could ever survive? But you offer forgiveness, that we might learn to fear you.
>
> —Psalm 130:3–4

Hurtful words, neglect, and downright dislike characterized Debbie Alsdorf's mother's influence on her entire life. As a result, seeds of insecurity and fear threatened to paralyze Debbie until her complete surrender to Christ began an inner healing process, a process she shares in her book *It's Momplicated: Hope and Healing for Imperfect Daughters of Imperfect Mothers.*

Debbie was determined to choose the godly response to all her mother dished out, and she maintained this for years and years. Even to the point of taking care of her elderly mother in her waning years of poor health. After a particularly scary near-death episode, Debbie knew she needed to ask the hard question.

"When you were in surgery, I was afraid that you would die and I would never know what was wrong—what was wrong with me . . . why couldn't you accept me? Why did you always say I messed up when I was trying so hard to be good?"[1] she inquired tearfully.

What unfolded from Debbie's mother was a sad, tragic story of a young woman married to an alcoholic—a wife who had saved up grocery

92

money to escape him. Until she found out she was pregnant. "I never wanted you. You spoiled my plan, and I resented you for that. I believed you had ruined my life. . . . When you were about six months old, I made a decision . . . I promised God that I would raise you and provide for you with every physical need, but I would not let you into my heart."[2] her mother replied.

Hearing this confession was a pivotal moment. Debbie was able to hold her mother and weep for the years that had been lost. They promised to make their remaining time together count. "It wasn't perfect, but I did get many 'I love yous.' A few months before she died, she even told me something I had never heard from her. She said I was pretty. . . . It was a moment I will never forget."[3]

Is there someone you need to forgive?

This person may or may not still be around or even be alive. But if there is a deep wound that was inflicted long ago or even yesterday, it is your choice to offer forgiveness. Your offender doesn't actually have to know you are releasing your right to have judgment. And there may not necessarily be a reconciliation, as there was with Debbie and her mother. But your choice will release you from that person's hold.

Debbie emphasizes that in choosing to forgive, "you are not excusing her for what she did—you are choosing to treat her with love. If you hold on to resentment and are unwilling to forgive her, the only person you are hurting is yourself. . . . Jesus offers forgiveness to everyone for the wrongs they have done, and we are taught to do the same."[4]

God has forgiven us much. But He also asks us to choose to forgive others. "In prayer there is a connection between what God does and what you do. You can't get forgiveness from God, for instance, without also forgiving others. If you refuse to do your part, you cut yourself off from God's part" (Matthew 6:14–15 *The Message*).

If we are to be His disciples, we must follow His example. If God will forgive our most relentless enemy, we can do nothing less. Jesus did not say that certain offenses are unworthy of our forgiveness. We have no biblical excuse for allowing unforgiveness in our hearts. —Henry Blackaby and Richard Blackaby, *Experiencing God Day by Day*[5]

We do not have to be women held back and defined by what was said or done to us in the past. Let's take the courageous step to release—for that is what forgiveness is—and walk in freedom.

> *Lord, You are the only one who knows exactly how much pain that person caused me—wounds that still affect me to this day. Would You please step in and give me the courage and strength to choose to forgive them so that I may be finally released into freedom? Amen.*

How Will I Choose Forgiveness?

_____

_____

_____

_____

_____

_____

_____

_____

_____

_____

_____

_____

_____

DAY 31

Choose to Believe

Worship Christ as Lord of your life. And if someone asks about your hope as a believer, always be ready to explain it.

—1 Peter 3:15

> What comes into our minds when we think about God is the most important thing about us. —A. W. Tozer, *The Knowledge of the Holy*[1]

At a recent state funeral at Washington National Cathedral, there was a moment in the Episcopal service where the congregation stood to recite the Apostles' Creed. On the very front row, two distinguished guests stood silently—obvious in their choice not to participate. Later ensued a barrage of social media commentary—most negative, some positive. The internet was full of comments about the Creed that merely showed how ignorant so many are today regarding matters of the faith.

Life really is all about what you believe.

That particular funeral was for a great man with deep faith in God, one who actually believed everything stated in the Apostles' Creed. At age twelve, in my own first public proclamation of a personal faith in Christ, I too recited the Apostles' Creed—and have been doing so ever since.

I believe in God, the Father almighty, creator of heaven and earth. I believe in Jesus Christ, his only Son, our Lord. He was conceived by the power of the Holy Spirit and born of the Virgin Mary. He suffered under Pontius Pilate, was crucified, died, and was buried. He descended to the dead. On the third day he rose again. He ascended into heaven, and is seated at the right hand of the Father. He will come again to judge the living and the dead. I believe in the Holy Spirit, the holy Catholic* church, the communion of saints, the forgiveness of sins, the resurrection of the body, and the life everlasting. Amen. —Apostles' Creed, c. AD 700 (*meaning the universal church)

These few words, dating from the early church, summarize the Christian faith. Think of a small acorn that contains all the elements of a large oak tree—that's the image of a short creed condensing into just a few words a belief system contained in both the Old and New Testaments of the Bible.

As the authentic and authorized summary of Christian truth, the creed is a symbol of the faith of the whole Church. . . . The creed was never meant to be a substitute for personal faith, for a trusting relationship with God. . . . We profess our faith not in the words but in the reality to which they point. Reciting the creed . . . reminds us of the truths of our salvation and gives us an opportunity to personally affirm them.[2]

What do you believe? It's important to know. And to, like Peter, "always be ready to explain it."

Some people find this conversation uncomfortable, perhaps because they have never made a clear confession of faith or received assurance of pardon. Or they believe in God but struggle with words to describe such.

Here is a simple prayer that can be offered even now in order to make your faith and beliefs sure—naming Jesus Christ as your Savior and Lord. *"Dear Jesus, thank You for loving me so much that You came to live among* us. *Please forgive my sins—all those times I've chosen my way and not Yours. Thank You for Your death and Resurrection, enabling me to live freely here and eternally with You in heaven. I invite You to make Your home in my heart and help me grow so I may serve and glorify You as Lord of my life forever. Amen."*

If you prayed that prayer or one similar at any time in your life, you are part of God's forever family. You belong to Him always—now and into eternity. And for those who are still searching to put your own beliefs into words and thoughts, be assured God is right beside you on this seeking journey of faith. My prayer is He will make His will and His way clear to you. Never forget how much He loves you and calls you His child.

This is what I believe.

Lord, sometimes I'm actually confused about what I do believe. Those who call themselves Christians occasionally say and do things I would never embrace. Yet You know I'm searching for deeper spiritual meaning in my life. Please show me the way. Amen.

How Will I Choose to Believe?

_____

_____

_____

_____

_____

_____

_____

_____

DAY 32

Choose Celebration

We had to celebrate this happy day. For your brother was dead and
has come back to life! He was lost, but now he is found!

—Luke 15:32

When we received two "You Are Special Today" red plates for wedding
gifts, I always intended to return one of them. At the time it never
occurred to me how I would use one, much less two.

Thirty-five years later I'm so thankful I never got around to that errand.
Those red plates have prompted countless celebrations in our home and
often for two people at a time!

There's just something truly, well, special about a table set with flowers, candles, cloth napkins in fun napkin holders, various glasses, cups, and
saucers, and beautiful red plates shouting out, "You Are Special Today."

Who wouldn't love to be recognized as the guest of honor?

For instance, our family tradition is that on someone's birthday they get
to pick the menu, and then while everyone is still at the table, we go around
and each tells the birthday girl or guy one thing we most appreciate about
them. When the kids were middle schoolers there were groans aplenty as
they fidgeted while listening to praise. But our eldest son (who is entirely
transparent) still beams and considers this the very best part of his birthday.
It's no wonder—his love language is words of encouragement!

Perhaps the best celebrations of all are those that take the guest of honor by surprise. Which is, of course, the story in our Scripture today. That prodigal son who ran away and squandered his inheritance seeking pleasure and people to purpose his life. But in failure, he reached the end of himself and ashamedly trudged home to the only place he knew, the very family he had abandoned.

I'm pretty sure the last thing he expected was a well-stocked dining table featuring a "You Are Special Today" red plate setting just for him! (Though maybe he wasn't surprised by a haughty elder brother standing by with indignation.) And yet this is exactly where we see his compassionate father make a choice for celebration. "We had to celebrate this happy day. For your brother was dead and has come back to life! He was lost, but now he is found!"

The pervading thought here is this guest of honor is welcome, worthy, and totally accepted. The emphasis seems to be on the generosity of the father rather than the sinfulness of the son. This is true celebration—total focus and acceptance of the guest of honor.

Brennan Manning, who often referred to himself as a ragamuffin prodigal, says, "The son had barely arrived on the scene when suddenly a fine new robe was thrown over his shoulders. He hears music, the fatted calf is being carried into the parlor, and he didn't even have a chance to say to his father, 'I'm sorry.' God wants us back even more than we could possibly want to be back. We don't have to go into great detail about our sorrow. All we have to do, the parable says, is appear on the scene, and before we get a chance to run away again, the Father grabs us and pulls us into the banquet."[1]

What are some small celebrations you could orchestrate in your own home and life?

Finished up that project at work (For writers, met that book deadline)

Survived the first one hundred days of the school year

Memorized a Bible verse or the words to a hymn or Christmas carol

Daylight Savings Time either started or ended

Kid came home from college for the weekend

It's finale night of your favorite TV show

You or a family member ran their first half-marathon

All the outside Christmas lights were put up

Just because it's Tuesday (or Thursday)

To celebrate a half-year birthday (or Christmas on July 25)

You get the idea. Celebrate anything and anyone because making ordinary days special is good for the soul!

The reason to celebrate is the person—who they are, what they've done, or even just because they are here! People will forget what your décor was, the menu, and what present you gave them, but they will always remember how they felt in your presence.

Lord, You love a good party, and so do I. And yes, it is even better when we are celebrating something surprising and undeserving. Help me to learn how to do this more and more so that I can spread Your joy and acceptance to those who need it most. Amen.

How Will I Choose Celebration?

_____

_____

_____

_____

_____

_____

_____

DAY 33

Choose Deep

> My counsel for you is simple and straightforward: Just go ahead with what you've been given. You received Christ Jesus, the Master; now *live* him. You're deeply rooted in him. You're well constructed upon him. You know your way around the faith. Now do what you've been taught. School's out; quit studying the subject and start *living* it! And let your living spill over into thanksgiving.
>
> —Colossians 2:6–7 *The Message*

*I*s your influence on others deep or wide?

Today's culture extols the wide reach. For people in my profession, worth is measured by how many followers we have on social media and how many people come to speaking events or purchase books. Megachurches are often considered more significant than small country chapels.

The time and investment it takes to go deep in another person's life—to have that kind of influence—is not so easily measured for the masses.

Leighton Ford was once a young man with incredible gifts of preaching and ministry, and so it was not at all surprising when he became a popular pastor, evangelist, and author. Married to Billy Graham's sister, Jean, he partnered with other twentieth-century Christian leaders and had a wide influence through large crusades.

I was privileged that my very first job out of seminary was on the editorial staff of the Lausanne Committee for World Evangelization, which Leighton also directed. I observed firsthand a man of devout faith and integrity. He and Jean were an encouragement to me when I was just getting started, trying to figure out God's call on my life (and now in their eighties, they continue to be gracious). Leighton's passion was for raising up leaders all around the world for kingdom work. And he did it well.

In the ensuing years I spent my ordinary days raising four children, serving with my husband in ministry, and writing articles and books. Leighton, meanwhile, buried his young adult son Sandy and began to reevaluate his own life. He released his responsibilities of the Lausanne Committee to others and decided to follow the nudge of the Holy Spirit in stepping out of the limelight and quietly investing in young men and women through spiritual mentoring.

In the midst of his own suffering, Leighton sensed God's clarification on what was most important—not conventional success but work done quietly and without fanfare. He chose deep.

One of those young men he discipled reflected recently:

Even though Leighton's new ministry was humble and obscure compared with his rock-star stadium evangelist status with the Billy Graham team, his original vision to make a difference in people's lives has been fulfilled in a beautiful and unexpected way. Over the decades Leighton has continued to walk with a small number of people in a deeper way as "an artist of the soul and a friend on the journey." And over time, the ripple effect of one dedicated life has been felt around the world, across generations, and into eternity. . . . His influence is deep and wide. And he is now at home in his own skin, truly content with his life and calling. —Ken Shigematsu, *Survival Guide for the Soul: How to Flourish Spiritually in a World that Pressures Us to Achieve*[1]

It takes courage to walk away from big. It takes a person who is absolutely confident in God's unconditional love and acceptance. One convinced that if God is calling them to be Jesus to the world, He will provide every opportunity for that to happen. Big ones. Small ones.

I believe it is a sign of security and contentment when we are able to embrace with joy the small opportunities—the one-on-one encounters— with as much enthusiasm as we celebrate the loud and large.

This is a goal for my current season of life. And, like Leighton, I am finding great meaning and purpose in going deep with a few—people whose names you don't know. Yet.

What is your own calling?

Mark Labberton, president of Fuller Seminary, says, "The vocation of every Christian is to live as a follower of Jesus today. In every aspect of life, in small and large acts, with family, neighbors and enemies, we are to seek to live out the grace and truth of Jesus. This is our vocation, our calling."[2]

That calling—that which we consider our first thing—never changes. But *how* our specific calling is manifested in varying details and seasons are next things, and they will evolve over our lifetime.

Jesus says to us as He did to each of His disciples, "Follow me" (Matthew 4:19). Be careful with your choice and your response—your influence has the potential to be both deep *and* wide.

Lord, I've always wanted my life to count for something—to make a difference in the world. I guess it's easier to see this happening when influence is wide. But my prayer today is You would help me choose to invest in deep and meaningful. Amen.

How Will I Choose Deep?

Choose Hello

All the friends here say hello. Pass the greetings around with holy embraces!

—1 Corinthians 16:20 *The Message*

I f you need to have blood drawn at 6 a.m., there's no better phleboto- mist than Maria. I discovered this after stumbling into her lab, eager to get the ordeal over with so I could break the fast and finally have my coffee.

A bit squeamish, it occurred to me that conversation might ease my mind off what she was doing to me. I said, "Hello, my name is Cindy. What's yours?"

After that quick exchange, the room got silent again, and the needle loomed large. Noticing a childlike drawing on the wall, I prompted, "Tell me about your child."

"Oh, that was colored by my daughter Christina. You saw her waiting out in the lobby. She doesn't get a ride to her work program until 8:30, so she comes here with me early in the morning."

I had seen a young adult woman busy playing games on a tablet. Sensing some special needs, I had greeted her briefly in my pre-coffee stupor.

As Maria began chatting about her daughter's struggles, I commiserated with her on various changing state policies for those with disabilities. "Maria, I have a young adult son who has intellectual disabilities, so I understand your frustration," I commented.

We then shared, as mamas tend to do, about the fun and funny things our kids do. She showed me a cell phone video of teaching her daughter how to use clothes pins on a clothesline in her apartment, and I laughed about the time we had to explain to Justin what "bald" was—that our elderly minister had not intentionally shaved his head.

We agreed that it seems the explanations never stop.

"I am so proud of Christina's twin who is now a special education teacher in Hartford," Maria declared. I agreed that this was quite an achievement. I've also seen my other children grasp a passion for the differently abled as well because of their experiences with their own brother.

Suddenly I glanced down and discovered eight full vials of my own red blood in her hands. That difficult deed had happened while I was caught up in meeting a new friend.

My simple act of connection had opened a door.

In preparing to leave, I turned to thank her and said, "Maria, these things are hard, but God is faithful and will help you every step of the way. I've lived longer than you, and I have seen so much goodness and grace come out of the struggles."

She hugged me tightly. The phlebotomist hugged me. I can honestly say that was a first. It was definitely my very best blood draw ever.

It's easy to wander through our daily errands incognito—never catching the eye of another person, holding back so we are not perceived as too forward, or even just avoiding conversation because it feels safer to stay incubated against the world.

But think of all the phenomenal people we miss! And think of those who miss the encouragement we have to offer as well.

Who will you encounter today in the normal rush of life? That stranger can actually become a real person before your very eyes if you take the time to say hello.

Sometimes you find an important point of connection. Sometimes you meet a sister.

Lord, please forgive me for all those times I looked beyond the person right in front of me. That one who served while I didn't even notice. Help me to focus on each person and to seek out their wisdom even as I embrace their worth as made in Your image. Amen.

How Will I Choose Hello?

_____

_____

_____

_____

_____

_____

_____

_____

_____

_____

_____

_____

_____

_____

_____

_____

Choose Stories

All Jesus did that day was tell stories—a long storytelling afternoon. His storytelling fulfilled the prophecy: I will open my mouth and tell stories; I will bring out into the open things hidden since the world's first day.

—Matthew 13:34–35 *The Message*

"Daddy, please tell us a story!" we begged.

We had just finished another supper of corn bread, Georgia field peas, baked ham, fresh tomato slices, and, of course, sweet iced tea. My sisters and I had cleared the dishes, and now came the time we eagerly awaited as we sat at the family table.

Which one would it be? The one about great-grandfather Pratt, an inventor who had the first car in Atlanta and kept the formula for Coca-Cola in his safe (for his buddy Asa Candler)? Or the one about Daddy's childhood pet frog Puddin' who croaked so long and loudly one night Grandfather shot him? Maybe we'd hear again of how sixteen-year-old Daddy wrote the manager of the Waldorf Astoria hotel in New York City and offered his high school band, The Stardusters, to play there—receiving a very polite letter declining the offer.

We didn't care which one he chose. We loved a good story, and Daddy told the best.

We also had family devotions around the table and heard other stories—of God's great love for a people who too often rejected Him, of saints and sinners all used by God to do incredible things, and of miracles, mangers, and meanderings through the wilderness.

And some nights Daddy pulled out his reel-to-reel tape recorder and thrust the microphone in our faces, "interviewing" us about life, our school activities, and urging us to recite a memorized poem or Scripture or song.

Is it any wonder I grew up loving stories?

I still do. Not only that, I'm grateful to be living a story, one that is totally unique and utterly unpredictable. But most of all, I rejoice that I'm part of God's great story of a kingdom that never ends. It is my deepest prayer that I will live my story with honor and be faithful to the end.

The world today is also enchanted with stories. We not only want to read a good book or watch a thrilling movie; we often become totally absorbed in the characters—both fictional and real. We're eager to see the plot resolved, journey completed, mystery solved, or lovers reconciled. Stories help us deal with life.

Story is the primary way in which the revelation of God is given to us. The Holy Spirit's literary genre of choice is story. . . . Moses told stories; Jesus told stories; the four Gospel writers presented their good news in the form of stories. And the Holy Spirit weaves all this storytelling into the vast and holy literary architecture that reveals God to us as Father, Son, and Holy Spirit in the way that he chooses to make himself known. . . . Story is the primary means we have for learning what the world is, and what it means to be a human being in it. No wonder that from the time we acquire the mere rudiments of language, we demand stories.
—Eugene Peterson, *Leap Over a Wall: Earthly Spirituality for Everyday Christians*[1]

We long for meaning in our ministry, purpose in our passion, and worth in our walk of faith. Our text today certainly reinforces the view that Jesus was a theologian who told stories. Eternal truths were communicated clearly through parables structured around everyday experiences such as planting seeds, borrowing money, or welcoming home a rebellious teenager.

Are you sharing your own stories—beginning at home with your family but also extending to anyone who will listen?

The world is full of people angrily spouting their opinions. The Internet is clogged with judgment and condemnation. But harsh tones turn off listeners. What people are longing to hear are *stories.* Of good triumphing over evil. Of the downtrodden who overcome great odds. Stories of adventure, truth, valor, and courage. Stories that draw us in and hint that perhaps even we could be like that person. Real stories of those who are broken just like us. But then they rise . . . They make discoveries and transform into more than they ever imagined. "No eye has seen, no ear has heard, and no mind has imagined what God has prepared for those who love him" (1 Corinthians 2:9).

How will the story of your life unfold? And when will you share it?

Let the redeemed of the LORD tell their story.

—Psalm 107:2 NIV

Lord, it's the stories we remember long after the sermon is over. Would You help me know how to share my own stories with others? So they too can understand Your part in the ups and downs of my own life and theirs? Amen.

How Will I Choose Stories?

_____

_____

_____

_____

_____

_____

Choose to Dwell

Dwell in Me, and I will dwell in you.

—John 15:4 AMPC

*I*t's a pretty remarkable promise, actually, "I will dwell in you." These words from Jesus, spoken to His friends and, by extension through Scripture, to each of us.

The word *dwell* is defined as where we *focus* and where we *live*. In essence today's text, "Dwell in Me," invites us to put all our focus on Jesus and to live with Him every minute of every day. But that's not even the most remarkable part of the verse—we are promised He will do the same for us! "I will dwell in you."

Where do you usually dwell?

Bombarded with endless demands for time and energy from people you love and people you don't? Surrounded by noise and chaos and hurry? Knee-deep in fear or insecurity—always wondering if you're enough?

Would you prefer to dwell in serenity and strength? This kind of life is actually possible—and you can choose it today.

We cannot underestimate the importance of this final conversation Jesus had with His closest friends as He walked with them on the path to the garden of Gethsemane. He wove a story of branches and vines, emphasizing how sustenance comes from being connected—grafted into the True Vine.

For a branch cannot produce fruit if it is severed from the vine, and you cannot be fruitful unless you remain in me. Yes, I am the vine; you are the branches. Those who remain in me, and I in them, will produce much fruit. For apart from me you can do nothing.

—John 15:4–5

This is the prerequisite for our bearing fruit—to remain in Him. And what can we accomplish solely in our own strength? Nothing.

> [Jesus] called the process "abiding," which is the same thing as dwelling. In fact, this command to abide was so significant that this word is repeated no less than eight times in John 15. Abiding in Christ is living out our union with Him in faith, baptism, love, obedience, and Eucharist. This image of vine and branches reveals that life flows from the Vine to the branches, indicating that our abiding in Christ is not static, but dynamic and vitalizing. —Lucinda Secrest McDowell, *Dwelling Places: Words to Live in Every Season*[1]

Whether we translate this verb in our text as *dwell* or *abide*, it stems from the Greek active imperative verb, indicating continual action. Not once and done, but for a lifetime.

One of my favorite Scottish hymns is "Abide with Me," written by Henry Lyte in 1847:

Abide with me: fast falls the eventide;
The darkness deepens; Lord, with me abide.
When other helpers fail and comforts flee,
Help of the helpless, O abide with me.

Will you make the choice each morning to dwell with Christ? And then, will you make the choice to abide at night when "fast falls the eventide"?

You and I are God's people. Let's cling to that promise always.

Look! God's dwelling place is now among the people, and he will dwell with them. They will be his people, and God himself will be with them and be their God.

—Revelation 21:3 NIV

Lord, I long for You to be my forever home—both the person and the place where I'm always enfolded. I recognize that nothing good can come from my life unless I abide in You—the source and nourishment for growth and grace. I'm ready to dwell forever. Amen.

How Will I Choose to Dwell?

_____

_____

_____

_____

_____

_____

_____

_____

_____

_____

_____

DAY 37

Choose to Think

Whatever is true, whatever is noble, whatever is right, whatever is pure, whatever is lovely, whatever is admirable—if anything is excellent or praiseworthy—think about such things.

—Philippians 4:8 NIV

All change begins in the mind. The Apostle Paul believed a person could be "transformed by the renewing of your mind" (Romans 12:2 NIV). Changed for better. Or changed for worse.

Recently these truths were fleshed out for me in a very real way. For nearly two years my husband noticed changes in both his body and mind. Determined to reclaim good health, if his walking seemed imbalanced, he went to more classes at the gym. If he found himself forgetful or confused, he tried to solve harder problems. When mobility and cognition continued to deteriorate, he visited numerous doctors and endured endless testing only to hear, "Just get used to this, it's all part of aging."

In reality, it was his brain—his mind—that was in trouble. And it took both a neurologist and neurosurgeon to finally diagnose NPH (normal pressure hydrocephalus), which explained the consequences of extreme pressure on parts of his brain. Fortunately, he was able to have a permanent shunt inserted to drain the cerebral spinal fluid, which we are hopeful will restore him to stronger health.

In Mike's case, these were things he could *not* control, but there are many we *can*. Scientists have recently confirmed what many of us have long embraced as biblical redemption—that we can actually *choose* the path our thoughts will take and rewire our brains.

In her book *Unsinkable Faith*, author Tracie Miles shares about some of the ways we can begin to rewire our brains and targets common areas where women struggle, including comparing, exaggerating, complaining, blaming, self-condemning thoughts, overthinking, maintaining a victim mentality, and dwelling in an all-is-lost mindset. How many of these clearly reflect your own thinking? And what would it take for you to instead embrace "whatever is true, whatever is noble, whatever is right, whatever is pure, whatever is lovely, whatever is admirable"?

Miles shares from expert Dr. Caroline Leaf who urges us to be proactive. Leaf says, "When you understand the power of your thought life, you truly begin to get a glimpse of how important it is to take responsibility for what you are thinking."[1]

Have you allowed negative thinking to take up valuable real estate in your brain?

Miles was further inspired by Dr. Daniel G. Amen and his *New York Times* best-selling book *Change Your Brain, Change Your Life*. Miles wrote that Amen not only points out the complexity of how God made our brains and the importance of brain health, but he "confirmed that it is possible to live a life filled with positive thinking, even for those of us who have spent years weighted down with hard circumstances, painful memories, crushed dreams, negativity, and generalized pessimism."[2] My Texas friend calls that "stinkin' thinkin.'"

Are you finally ready to do something about your thought life?

You know that pessimism that seems to invade your brain, especially when you are tired or stressed or feeling insecure? Dr. Amen refers to such as ANTs—automatic negative thoughts. And just like little ants crawling all over the ground, they will multiply unless we crush them at the onset. Reject and then replace them with life-giving words and actions.

> The choices we make about which thoughts we allow and which we reject will drive our attitude and dictate our overall happiness. When we commit to . . . noticing negative thoughts, rejecting them, and replacing them with new thoughts—we take control of our thinking and our overall health and happiness. That's a lot of power God has put at our disposal![3]

Choose today to "take captive every thought to make it obedient to Christ" (2 Corinthians 10:5 NIV).

> *Lord, thank You for creating me with a mind that can think and choose. Please continue to give me wisdom in all my pursuits and values. I want to focus on that which brings life, not that which crushes a spirit and soul. I choose to follow Your lead today. Amen.*

How Will I Choose to Think?

_____

_____

_____

_____

_____

_____

_____

_____

_____

_____

Choose Calm

A gentle answer deflects anger, but harsh words make tempers flare.

—Proverbs 15:1

*T*he kids were fighting again.

Author Tricia Goyer had a storm going on in her home, and she often didn't know where to turn. She wrote, "Some days I questioned whether anything would change, and I feared that the future would just get worse not better. Some days I wanted to lock my bedroom door, curl up on my floor, and hide. Most days I'd give anything—anything—for one day of calm."[1]

Though I don't have ten kids like Tricia does, I did raise four, including one with special needs. And I remember being desperate to know how to bring a calming presence into our home. Because too often I was not calm. Sibling arguments and frustrating challenges would set me off. I'd be panicked in how to be what that child most needed and, in my fear of doing the wrong thing, I would overreact. Often in a harsh tone. And sadly, a mama's fear can sometimes sound like anger.

Do you need to get a better handle on calm?

As I prayed for God to change me into a woman not so easily ruffled, I discovered I truly could *choose* to speak in soft tones, words that were soothing and calm. Even when my son was screaming out of frustration. Whereas two loud people only fuel the fire, if one tones down, quite often the other follows. Our text today is so true—"a gentle answer deflects anger."

If you are also looking for ways to establish calm in your chaos, I would like to share a new-to-me term, *affect labeling*, which is the process of listening to another person's emotional experience and reflecting back those emotions in short, simple "you" statements. Tricia Goyer confirms, "When a child knows you recognize his emotions and are paying attention, he feels heard. . . . One of the best ways to help our kids feel heard—and to de-escalate the situation—is to label their emotions."[2]

Tricia recalls a particular situation when her girls were yelling at each other:

Intervening, she began, *"You are angry."* "Yes. I'm angry. She's always getting into my stuff."

"You are frustrated." "Yes, because I already told her that if she needs something to just ask."

"You feel unloved." "Yes, I wish she would just really think about me and not just herself."

Her daughter then became more relaxed and calmer, realizing Tricia paid attention to her emotions. Not only that, but her sibling overheard what her actions were doing to her sister. This mama helped her child name her emotions, which is the first step to dealing with them in a calm manner.

An expert on affect labeling explains, "Unlike with other forms of reflective listening, when you wish to calm someone down, you must ignore the words and pay attention to the emotions. This is counterintuitive to many people. We are trained to pay attention to words . . . we do not learn how to listen for emotions."[3]

I can only be a calming presence—in my home, workplace, or wider community—when I have first calmed myself, as the psalmist clearly states, "I have calmed and quieted myself, like a weaned child who no longer cries for its mother's milk. Yes, like a weaned child is my soul within me" (Psalm 131:2).

How do you calm and quiet yourself?

Somehow, I doubt the old counting-to-ten thing is very effective any more. Perhaps this is why our Lord tells us to spend time daily with Him in prayer, Scripture, and peaceful silence, soothing music, a cup of strong, hot tea, or a long walk in the woods. It is not selfish to take care of our souls—in fact, it may just be the healthiest investment in our relationships. Because we have invested in time apart, when we do come together with others, we bring a person who is calm and whole.

Next time you find yourself flustered and unsettled (whether it be with children, people in leadership, or yourself) try to pinpoint the emotions you are feeling at the time. Listen for God's words to you through His written Word, and speak kindness and understanding over yourself and others.

Lord, I long for calm in both my home and my heart. Help me identify emotions (mine and others') so I may take steps toward understanding and communication. Keep my voice soft and my soul nourished so I may offer grace-filled reconciliation. Amen.

How Will I Choose Calm?

_____

_____

_____

_____

_____

_____

_____

_____

_____

_____

Choose Grace

For God saved us and called us to live a holy life. He did this, not because we deserved it, but because that was his plan from before the beginning of time—to show us his grace through Christ Jesus.

—2 Timothy 1:9

In 1995 the world held its collective breath, awaiting the results of the O. J. Simpson trial for the murder of his ex-wife and her friend—often called the most publicized criminal trial in history.

I was in a staff meeting when the results were reported to us: acquittal.

I confess my immediate thought was, "That man will not get what he deserves."

And then, to my shock, I clearly heard the voice of God, "Neither do you, Cindy, neither do you."

Grace is God giving us what we don't deserve and can never earn. And can never lose.

It is simply and purely a gift. But one we must actively receive and incorporate into our lives. I lived a long time without unwrapping my gift of grace. Oh, I knew I was saved and I was seeking to live under the lordship of Christ, but I hadn't yet fully grasped my great sinfulness . . . or His great love and forgiveness. Of me.

The very nature of grace is that it is undeserved.

If we earned it, grace would be a reward—for good behavior, for doing all the right things—sort of like brownie points. For people who live in a culture full of reward and punishment, the concept of undeserved grace doesn't come easily. Because I could not grasp it, I became a POW—prisoner of works. I thought if I *did* enough, God would *love* me more.

Are you trying to *do* enough and *be* enough to earn God's favor? Aren't you ready to just lay it all down—all the striving and stressing? Will you just pick up the gift of grace and open it?

In Victor Hugo's classic novel *Les Misérables*, Jean Valjean commits the crime of stealing a loaf of bread to feed his hungry family. An act that ultimately sends him to prison for nineteen long years. By the time he is released, it is a bitter man who wanders for days, unable as a former convict to find shelter. Until a kind bishop offers him a room.

However, in the middle of the night, Jean Valjean steals the bishop's silver and sneaks away, only to be caught by the authorities. As they deliver him to the bishop's door and show the stolen silver, what Jean Valjean deserved was *punishment* for his criminal act.

What he receives instead is *grace*. The bishop exclaims, "I am glad to see you. Well, but how is this? I gave you the candlesticks too, which are of silver like the rest, and for which you can certainly get two hundred francs. Why did you not carry them away with your forks and spoons?"[1]

Then the bishop assures the policemen the silver was his gift to Valjean. And after the officers leave, as the bishop sends Valjean on his way, he charges him to use the money from selling the silver to turn his life around.

The rest of the story reveals the utter transformation that takes place in the life of this man. Because of his experience at being the recipient of such a gift, Valjean literally spends the rest of his life doling out large portions of grace to those around him. Javert, who was a guard at Valjean's prison and later became an inspector, couldn't understand it any more than our own world, which doesn't understand when we live out God's unfolding grace.

When we choose to live as those who have received grace, we are compelled to make a choice to offer grace. To everyone.

What does that look like? A hundred small and large things. Mostly, it looks like wounded healers. Those of us who walk with a limp are slower and more approachable to the hurting ones seeking healing. It looks like seeing beyond what is being said to what is going on in another person's heart, their life, their circumstances. Not taking offense. It means living for an audience of one—doing all to the glory of God.

Grace changed my life forever, and it can change yours too.

> *Lord, You know how much time and effort I wasted striving to be perfect. Thank You for offering the gift of grace to all of us who are completely unworthy but totally accepted. Help me, in turn, become a grace-giver to those I encounter who need to know the good news. Amen.*

How Will I Choose Grace?

_____

_____

_____

_____

_____

_____

_____

_____

_____

_____

_____

_____

Choose Power

For the Kingdom of God is not just a lot of talk; it is living by God's power.

—1 Corinthians 4:20

She had no idea she had any power. All she thought she had was beauty. And a big secret.

Esther was a Jewish orphan living in Persia with her cousin Mordecai. The Bible tells us she was so beautiful that when King Xerxes was looking for a new queen, "she won his favor and approval" (Esther 2:17 NIV). So he put a crown on it.

Though she'd won the love of Xerxes and earned the trust of her court attendants, Esther neglected to tell her new husband she was Jewish. After all, her people were in danger of annihilation due to the vengeance of Xerxes's right-hand man, Haman.

Since Queen Esther was firmly established in the palace, her cousin Mordecai begged her to intervene with the king and save the Jews from Haman's attacks. "Who knows but that you have come to your royal position for such a time as this?" (Esther 4:14 NIV).

It was time for an important choice to be made, and this queen knew her only power resided in God. So Esther's immediate response was to ask the Jews to fast and pray with her, "When this is done, I will go to the king, even though it is against the law. And if I perish, I perish" (v. 16 NIV).

When was the last time you were asked to do something for which you felt unprepared? Did you recoil in fear or go forth in Holy Spirit power?

God immediately answered Esther's prayers—granting strength and courage to face her king and gain his favor even though she entered his presence unbidden, an act normally punishable by death. She used her audience with the king to reveal Haman's true plan against the Jews and entreated Xerxes to save her people with a royal edict. He not only gave her what she asked, but he punished Haman's deceit by hanging, and he elevated Mordecai to rule his household.

Most importantly, God's people were saved, and to this day the Jews celebrate Esther's role through the annual feast of Purim. "In every province and in every city to which the edict of the king came, there was joy and gladness among the Jews, with feasting and celebrating" (Esther 8:17 NIV).

God uses women to help bring about His kingdom through "living by God's power." This is why we were created.

In the biblical account of creation (Genesis 2), after God created man, Scripture records, "But still there was no helper just right for him" (v. 20). The original Hebrew language used for the word *helper* is *ezer*, which can either mean "strong helper," as God is a strong helper, or "strong power."

In the book *Reclaiming Eve*, the authors suggest the original meaning of this verse might be, "To end the loneliness of the single human, I will make another strong power, corresponding to it, facing it, equal to it. And the humans will be both male and female."[1]

That's what you are, sister, a strong power!

For not only has God identified you as his image-bearer, but he also chose back in the garden of Eden to identify you as a strong power. Nowhere in these two primary keys that unlock your identity do we find a hint of female inferiority or a whiff of male superiority. Instead, we find the beauty of an interdependent relationship formed by a God of relationship.[2]

Will you choose to say yes for such a time as this?

> *Lord, I realize the line between seeking power for my own glory and seeking power to enable me to glorify You are two different pursuits. Help me to be courageous and strong, discerning when and how to move forward in confidence and competence through You alone. Amen.*

How Will I Choose Power?

_____

_____

_____

_____

_____

_____

_____

_____

_____

_____

_____

_____

_____

_____

_____

_____

Choose Self-Care

Then Jesus said, "Let's go off by ourselves to a quiet place and rest awhile." He said this because there were so many people coming and going that Jesus and his apostles didn't even have time to eat.

—Mark 6:31

Perhaps it's been overused, but I still love the visual illustration from flight attendants who remind those traveling with little children that, in the event of an emergency, the adult should put their own oxygen mask on first.

How can we be of any use to others unless we first remain healthy?

In today's verse, it's clear even our Lord embraced this principle—self-care is necessary in order to be restored and equipped for the tasks ahead. Immediately following that season of withdrawal and strengthening came the feeding of the five thousand!

Do you regularly practice self-care?

We are not Wonder Woman. We are finite, imperfect people with limitations of time and energy. No matter the season. Even women with youthful strength and vigor also need to come to terms with boundaries.

One woman's own struggle with balance, joy, and motherhood prompted her to survey more than four hundred moms, asking for their insights about finding balance and practicing self-care while raising kids.

The common thread for everyone? *You can't neglect self-care.* This woman, Julie Burton, author of *The Self-Care Solution*, says, "As moms, we have an enormous opportunity to set a great example for our children of how to be kind to ourselves, and in turn, how to be kind to others. As the saying goes, we can't pour from an empty cup."[1]

So how do we keep our cups full? While solutions may certainly vary depending on age, status, and season of life, most of us know these basic choices for self-care:

- Stay connected to special friends and family.
- Get enough sleep—take short naps as necessary.
- Don't skip meals—eat and drink healthily.
- Keep regular appointments with your doctor and dentist.
- Move your body—take the steps.
- Keep growing intellectually—reading and listening.
- Feed your creativity in whatever fulfills you.
- Nourish your soul and spiritual life.

I know you probably have more you want to do and be than you can possibly accomplish in one lifetime. Believe me, so do I. From the vantage point of age, I can truthfully attest that putting a daily appointment with God on your calendar (preferably early morning) will reap long-term benefits. Time in Scripture and conversation in prayer with the One who knows you best and loves you most will fill up your soul for all the unexpected demands the day brings.

In 2 Corinthians 4:16 (NIV) Paul reminds us, "Though outwardly we are wasting away, yet inwardly we are being renewed day by day." Soul care is an important part of self-care. As a prayer from the thirteenth century goes—may we "see Thee more clearly, love Thee more dearly, follow Thee more nearly, day by day."

Pastor April Yamasaki reinforces the importance of soul care in her book *Four Gifts*, which focuses on care for heart, soul, mind, and strength. In a post on her blog she shares, "Though outward progress might elude us, though we might seem to be going backwards at times, yet things are not what they seem. Inwardly, we are being renewed by God's care day by day, and there is eternal glory ahead. So, do not lose heart."[2]

Start with one good choice today.

> *Lord, I do want to take care of myself, but everything else seems to demand my immediate attention. Help me follow the example of Jesus who chose time alone and apart in order to refuel for the work ahead of Him. May I choose You daily. Amen.*

How Will I Choose Self-Care?

_____

_____

_____

_____

_____

_____

_____

_____

_____

_____

_____

_____

_____

_____

Choose to Vote

Choose for each of your tribes individuals who are wise, discerning, and reputable to be your leaders.

—Deuteronomy 1:13 NRSV

*T*oday's Scripture affirms that Christ-followers have a biblical responsibility to our communities. So please don't complain about the condition of our country, government, or elected officials. If you don't vote.

It's easy to become complacent, easy to take some hard-won rights and privileges for granted. For instance, we've never lived during a time in the United States when only white male property owners were allowed to have a voice in the running of this country. But thankfully, brave women and men opened the doors for us all.

Will we walk through them?

The women's suffrage movement took activists and reformers nearly one hundred years to win the vote, and their campaign was wrought with much conflict. But when the 19th Amendment to the Constitution was ratified on August 26, 1920, it declared American women deserved all the rights and responsibilities of citizenship, equal to men.

Your vote and mine do make a difference. President Franklin Roosevelt reminded us to "never forget that government is ourselves and not an alien power over us. The ultimate rulers of our democracy are not a President and senators and congressman and government officials, but the voters of this country."

As citizens, voting is our right and privilege. As believers, we have a biblical precedent to choose "individuals who are wise, discerning, and reputable to be your leaders."

But it can be tempting to feel our vote doesn't really matter.

One vote gave statehood to California, Idaho, Oregon, Texas, and Washington. Frankly I can't even imagine a country without those significant states! In 1876 Rutherford B. Hayes beat Samuel J. Tilden for nineteenth president of the United States *by one electoral college vote*. I believe only time will reveal the difference our votes made throughout life.

Perhaps you did vote. But your candidate was not the one elected. This time. Will you despair, or will you choose to embrace these three truths?

God is still sovereign. He is not wringing His hands over any election. He is in control.

God reigns above the nations, sitting on his holy throne. —Psalm 47:8

LORD, God of our ancestors, you alone are the God who is in heaven. You are ruler of all the kingdoms of the earth. You are powerful and mighty; no one can stand against you! —2 Chronicles 20:6

We are called to pray regularly for our leaders and our country. Prayer is powerful.

The first thing I want you to do is pray. Pray every way you know how, for everyone you know. Pray especially for rulers and their governments to rule well so we can be quietly about our business of living simply, in humble contemplation. This is the way our Savior God wants us to live. —1 Timothy 2:1–3 *The Message*

God offers a purpose and a hope for us now and for generations in the years to come.

I make known the end from the beginning, from ancient times, what is still to come. I say, "My purpose will stand, and I will do all that I please." —Isaiah 46:10 NIV

How great are his signs, how mighty his wonders! His kingdom is an eternal kingdom; his dominion endures from generation to generation. —Daniel 4:3 NIV

I will not give up on my hopes for a country of strength, mercy, and goodwill to all. Voting is one way I can tangibly participate in change.

One day when your children ask you about this time in history, be sure you tell them that you made a deliberate choice to exercise your right to vote.

Lord, I know You call me to be in the world but not of the world. Being a good citizen of my home country is one way I can honor You and set an example of making good choices. Please guide me every step of the way, and keep me prayerful and positive. Amen.

How Will I Choose to Vote?

_____

_____

_____

_____

_____

_____

_____

_____

_____

_____

_____

_____

Choose Courage

This is my command—be strong and courageous! Do not be afraid or discouraged. For the LORD your God is with you wherever you go.

—Joshua 1:9

*E*unice loved her sister Rosemary and didn't always understand why the family kept Rosemary from numerous social events and school. But what pained Eunice the most was the fact Rosemary was unable to participate in all the family sport games surrounding their lives on Cape Cod in Massachusetts.

She was simply too "different." Yet this child was both created and loved by God.

One day Eunice made a choice to not only applaud her sister's unique qualities but also create a level playing field for folks just like Rosemary. She courageously chose to follow her vision of a different world where such people would be able to compete in sports, experiencing both teamwork and victory. So Eunice Kennedy Shriver started the Special Olympics in 1968, an international organization that has grown to over five million athletes in 174 countries.

Just over a decade after it began, I was a new mama taking night classes at the University of Washington on how to advocate for my special-needs son. Honestly, I was often overwhelmed. Learning Justin was the eligible age for Special Olympics, we enrolled him in track and field.

Little did I know how much that decision would totally change his life. And ours.

In his first competition I waited with open arms at the finish line as a "hugger," a designated volunteer position in those early years. I will never forget the joy on his face at finishing that race—perhaps the first time in his life he had been cheered by crowds! I still keep that photograph as a reminder that the little boy who once needed daily physical therapy is now a world-class athlete, in large part due to Special Olympics.

Yes, our son was born with intellectual disabilities. But I prefer to use "differing abilities," and believe me, if you knew Justin and his fellow athletes, I think you'd agree. Truly, they are all winners just by showing up—overcoming the naysayers in life and sometimes beating the medical, educational, or vocational odds. With courage.

Eunice Kennedy Shriver loved inspiring the athletes. During a speech at the 1981 Special Olympics she said, "What you are winning by your courage is far greater than any game. You are winning life itself and in so doing, you give to others a most precious prize . . . faith in the unlimited possibilities of the human spirit."

Is there someone special in your circle? Are you often unsure how to incorporate them into community events, family gatherings, and even church fellowship? Why not ask God to help you make some courageous, creative choices as Eunice did?

Your own courage is the first step in honoring that other person as one made in the image of God, created for a purpose. Yes, Special Olympics opened many doors for our Justin as he competed internationally and won medals in several sports. But it was the life lessons in endurance, commitment, sportsmanship, flexibility, traveling, and teamwork that have helped to make him the man he is today.

Perhaps the Special Olympics oath offers courage to everyone: "Let me win. But if I cannot win, let me be brave in the attempt."

Lord, different is sometimes scary to me. But I desire to get beyond my fears and reach out in help and empowerment to those who are struggling in our society. Please help me reach out with understanding and courage. We can make the world a better place for all. Amen.

How Will I Choose Courage?

_____

_____

_____

_____

_____

_____

_____

_____

_____

_____

_____

_____

_____

_____

_____

_____

_____

_____

Choose Friendship

A sweet friendship refreshes the soul.

—Proverbs 27:9 *The Message*

Make new friends, but keep the old. One is silver, and the other gold. A ring is round, it has no end. That's how long I will be your friend," we sang as Girl Scouts in the Brownie program gathered in a circle. Of course, we closed the meeting with the traditional daisy chain hand squeeze.

Though my adolescence was often fraught with relationship drama, I still see some of those dear *gold* hometown friends, even now with many, many years and miles between us. But I have also been blessed with *silver* friends—new people who have entered my life for a season or even a lifetime.

Friendship is best as a mutual relationship—one in which both parties find interests, companionship, and shared activities to be beneficial and life-giving. We discover potential friends almost anywhere we encounter people. It helps if we are inquisitive and truly interested in finding out about another's life. If we have to work too hard to make connections happen, perhaps it's not a good fit.

But what is a true soul friend? C. S. Lewis makes an observation that certainly rings true to me: "Friendship . . . is born at the moment when one man says to another "What! You too? I thought that no one but myself . . . "[1]

Interpersonal infrastructure is rapidly weakening. We find ourselves at the mercy of our devices—"on" constantly but not necessarily interacting with other humans in real time. We have thousands of followers but few true friends, and the isolation is taking a toll.

What is it about friendship that is so essential for women?

One psychologist believes that everyone has a desire to know and be known. She says, "Being created in the image of God, we've been designed for sociability, to be connected to God and interconnected together in unity, functioning as 'the body' of Christ. . . . Research findings show a connection between *close relationships* and *better coping skills* when confronted by stress, trauma, loss, and illness. Love and intimacy have healing qualities. There is value in friendship. . . . We do better together—sharing in bearing one another's burdens and rejoicing in celebrations. The support of others can ease devastation and disappointment and open up the possibility for healing and happier living."[2]

Our friends change us. And we change them as well.

Where can you find true friendship? Or would the better question be *how can I be a true friend*?

Start with a genuine interest in getting to know that new acquaintance—yes, questions, but also shared experiences. Try to look beyond the surface. Resist putting them in a category based on first impressions or assumptions. Be willing to share part of yourself—wisely. At your first coffee together, you may exchange favorite books, but you may not necessarily share your deepest fears (or you *may*).

As friendship develops, look for give and take. If you are always the one to initiate, maybe they aren't ready to invest the necessary time and energy at this point. But yet again, look beyond the surface—it could be an especially challenging season for that person, one rendering decisions and planning almost impossible. As your friendship grows, there will be times when they carry you as well.

Grace is always the best formula for friendships.

Sometimes I fail as a friend. I am guilty of neglect or insensitivity, and I have to admit it and ask forgiveness. Sometimes friends transition out of my life for a whole variety of reasons. Sometimes I put up walls, because people have used me in the past and I don't want to get hurt.

> And then someone enters our life who isn't looking for someone to use, is leisurely enough to find out what's really going on is us, is secure enough not to exploit our weaknesses or attack our strengths, recognizes our inner life and understands the difficulty of living out our inner convictions, confirms what's deepest within us. A friend. —Eugene Peterson, *Leap Over a Wall: Earthly Spirituality for Everyday Christians*[3]

Be that person today.

> *Lord, I'm so very grateful I don't have to do this life alone. Thank You for those sisters who listen, understand, and urge me to be better than I could ever have dared on my own. Help me be a caring and encouraging friend—perhaps to someone I might meet today. Amen.*

How Will I Choose Friendship?

_____

_____

_____

_____

_____

_____

_____

Choose Tears

Those who plant in tears will harvest with shouts of joy. They weep as they go to plant their seed, but they sing as they return with the harvest.

—Psalm 126:5–6

*H*ave you seen the popular romantic film *The Holiday*? In it, the character Amanda (played by Cameron Diaz) is a young woman who hasn't been able to cry for years. She simply shut down emotionally as a defense mechanism to keep up a strong façade. Although when she finally wants to cry, nothing succeeds in turning on the waterworks until she meets a certain widower. When it appears she has lost him and begins to weep involuntarily, that's when Amanda knows it must be *true love*.

The ability to cry tears is part of how our Creator made us. In fact, research demonstrates women cry at least four times as often as men because there is a clear correlation between hormones and tear production. Having more prolactin makes us better producers of tears. Well, honey, that explains a lot!

Modern culture sometimes looks askance at people bursting into tears. But the saints of old saw crying as a grace gift. They called it the *charism of tears*—the compassionate act of crying with someone in their distress.

I'm reminded of the little girl who was late getting home from school and had to answer her worried mama's question, "Why are you so late?"

"I had to help another girl who was sad," her daughter replied.

"What did you do to help her?" asked the mama.

"Oh, I just sat down and cried with her," said the little girl, totally unaware she had offered her friend a *charism of tears.*

When we choose to enter into another's pain, we are offering a precious gift of empathy and compassion.

Tears are also the price we pay for loving. I discovered this truth years ago when my lifetime best friend committed suicide, leaving me a note. I literally cried for days, like David. "My tears have been my food day and night, while people say to me all day long, 'Where is your God?'" (Psalm 42:3 NIV). My crying was a catharsis of sorts on a path I had never expected. Eventually, I—and most importantly her family—found the strength to move forward.

A godly older woman once gave me good advice concerning my tears: "Allow tears to flow. Scientists tell us they wash toxic chemicals from our bodies. Psychologists say they wash pain out of our hearts. . . . Crying buckets of tears is a journey. It takes us from where we were before loss to where we'll be once we've adapted to the changes loss brings."[1]

Who would have ever thought tears could be a vessel of renewal?

And yet today's text says, "Those who plant in tears will harvest with shouts of joy " But there is a caveat—we must carry seed to plant when we go out weeping. We must not see our tears as an end but as a means to know God's restoration. Then we sing as we return with the harvest.

When Jerry Sittser lost his wife, his mother, and one of his children in an automobile accident, he discovered how the soul can grow through tears and loss. He said, "I did not go through pain and come out the other side; instead, I lived in it and found within that pain the grace to survive and eventually grow. I did not get over the loss of my loved ones; rather, I absorbed the loss into my life, like soil receives decaying matter, until it became a part of who I am. Sorrow took up permanent residence in my soul and enlarged it. . . . I picked up a paintbrush and began, with great hesitation and distress, to paint a new portrait of our lives."[2]

Even Jesus wept (John 11:35). He weeps when we weep, and I believe one day He will make clear the meaning and purpose behind every tear.

Lord, I didn't realize crying could be a good thing, a cathartic and caring experience. May I never be ashamed of tender feelings that cause tears to flow freely. Keep my heart sensitive to those in pain and allow me to sometimes be a healing presence. Amen.

How Will I Choose Tears?

_____

_____

_____

_____

_____

_____

_____

_____

_____

_____

_____

_____

_____

_____

Day 46

Choose True Beauty

You should clothe yourselves instead with the beauty that comes from within, the unfading beauty of a gentle and quiet spirit, which is so precious to God.

—1 Peter 3:4

When she posted on social media, she immediately became a sensation. But for all the wrong reasons.

The photo of Crystal Hodges Johnson showed her face after a medical treatment for her port-wine stain birthmark, emphasizing a face that was swollen and purple. Definitely not the usual portrait of what is considered beauty. After discovering that several groups posted her image (without her permission) causing it to go viral to more than 30 million strangers around the world, she felt angry and hurt.

"I don't mind my story getting out there; I blog about my facial difference on a regular basis." Crystal writes. But she doesn't want sympathy. "I want my story to be known in attempts of educating other people, and in hopes of motivating a cultural change in how 'different' people are treated."[1]

I recently met this remarkable young woman at the Mount Hermon Christian Writers Conference in California where she received the True Grit Award. Awarded annually to someone who writes in the face of a daunting challenge while displaying godly character, a thankful spirit, and growth, Crystal beamed as she received a standing ovation.

Crystal is on the front lines of changing our culture's understanding of true beauty. She says, "My worth, beauty and value are so much deeper than what happens in the digital world. We're all different in our own ways—whether our differences are visible or not. But more than that? We're all beautiful and special in our own ways. We are more than the pixels that people see on their screens, and we can't allow others to make us believe otherwise."[2]

Our world is obsessed with outward beauty—that which we can see or touch or fantasize about, even if it's totally glossed over or fabricated digitally. And yet God's Word emphasizes we should pursue the "beauty that comes from within, the unfading beauty of a gentle and quiet spirit."

It takes more than a glance to get to know this kind of beauty in a person. It takes face-to-face, real-life time and effort. And that's a good thing. Fortunately, there are people willing to look beyond the surface. Crystal recently posted photographs from her wedding. I smiled and thanked God for her deliberate choice to live a full and balanced life, even though people often perceive her as less-than.

Cindy Sproles's award-winning novel, *Liar's Winter*, achingly reveals how the nineteenth-century Appalachian culture treated a young woman with port-wine stains—Lochiel was shunned and referred to as having the "devil's mark." But she never forgot what an older woman said to her, "We choose what we make ourselves to be. We can be kind or we can be meaner than a rattler."[3]

Lochiel realized she had to fix herself first, "I wanted my hate and anger gone, and I wanted to be kind—to choose to see the good in even them folks who wasn't so good."[4] This book was a hauntingly redemptive tale of a woman who chose to overcome the prejudice of her life and times through the choices she made.

Frankly I think we are all being played. We've been led to believe there's only one version of beauty. But we don't have to stay there! And there are some promising signs. When clothing company OshKosh B'gosh chose Asher and baby food company Gerber chose Lucas—both boys with Down syndrome—to represent their company image, a big step forward was made in depicting beauty and worth in a fresh way.

Perhaps Mama was right all along when she said, "It's what's inside that counts," and, "Pretty is as pretty does."

Rather than striving to *look* beautiful today, why don't we seek to *be* beautiful?

Lord, like most women, I long to be perceived as beautiful. But even as that concept is thankfully changing, so are my expectations. May I embrace my hard-won smile lines and scars that reveal the incredible life I've been given so far. Help me shine from deep within. Amen.

How Will I Choose True Beauty?

_____

_____

_____

_____

_____

_____

_____

_____

_____

_____

_____

_____

_____

Choose Battle

For we are not fighting against flesh-and-blood enemies, but against evil rulers and authorities of the unseen world, against mighty powers in this dark world, and against evil spirits in the heavenly places.

—Ephesians 6:12

I don't consider myself controversial. I speak. I write. I challenge people to go deeper in their faith with the God who gives them grace and mercy. My style is approachable, content-driven, and humorous even when I don't mean to be. Before I speak, I always pray God will use me—but I don't consider this living-on-the-edge kind of work. Certainly not dangerous.

In reality, I go to battle daily.

This was made very real to me while speaking on Cape Cod a dozen years ago—a lovely women's church event where my topic was "Tea and Friendship." As I stood to begin, a woman from the middle of the crowd stood large and tall, loudly screaming angry, nasty, accusatory words at me—maligning my character, my witness, and my integrity.

I was paralyzed with shock!

But almost immediately I realized she was someone retaliating for the fact I had been a witness in a trial on the Cape two years earlier. While the legal judgments had been served and resolved, the acrimony and hate had evidently lingered.

Within seconds, the Holy Spirit filled my shaking body, and I burst forth, leading the crowd in singing Martin Luther's strong words from his hymn "A Mighty Fortress Is Our God," "And though this world, with devils filled, should threaten to undo us, we will not fear, for God hath willed His truth to triumph through us. The Prince of Darkness grim, we tremble not for him, his rage we can endure, for lo, his doom is sure. One little word shall fell him."

By the final verse, the police had come and taken the heckler away, in deference to an existing restraining order. I took a deep breath, and then another. And when I couldn't stop my racing heart, I finally said, "Let's pray."

I then did what God had called me there to do in the first place. I gave my talk on "Tea and Friendship." Words of encouragement and hope were shared as well as tea and treats. Who would have thought my support for my dearest friend (by testifying at her trial) would be the most significant, unspoken illustration of my subject that night?

And I have never forgotten—not even for a day—that I am in battle against the enemy of my soul. Do you realize that you are too?

Satan wants to win. He wants to make your life so miserable, so full of fear, confusion, worry, and doubt, that you will simply become paralyzed and unable to move forward in any kind of productive or redeeming way. If he can immobilize you, if he can demoralize you, if he can distract you from being strong and serene in Christ, then he will have accomplished his purpose.

The villain in my story often whispers words that cause me to think I'm unworthy, doubt God's calling, or shame me into silence. His worst lie? *Nothing will ever change.*

He calls good evil and evil good and always helps us question whether God has anything good in mind in his plans for us. . . . Our experience of life deteriorates from the passion of a grand love affair, in the midst of a life-and-death battle, to an endless series of chores and errands, a busyness that separates us from God [and] each other. —John Eldredge, *The Sacred Romance: Drawing Closer to the Heart of God*[1]

How do you summon strength to hold onto what you know is true and real? You go into battle.

In his letter to the Ephesians, Paul lists the spiritual armor available to us: the belt of truth, body armor of righteousness, sandals of peace, shield of faith, helmet of salvation, and sword of the Spirit, God's Word. (See Ephesians 6:14–18.)

Will you choose to be armed for battle? Together, let's summon the courage to rise up and fight for ourselves and for others, by never forgetting that the King of kings is leading us on and preparing the way.

> I will go before you and will level the mountains; I will break down gates of bronze and cut through bars of iron. I will give you hidden treasures, riches stored in secret places, so that you may know that I am the LORD, the God of Israel, who summons you by name.
>
> —Isaiah 45:2–3 NIV

Let's go, warrior princess!

> *Lord, I much prefer seeking to be a woman of peace than a warrior princess. Yet I realize evil is real, and I must be vigilant and victorious over that which stands in my way of living fully and faithfully. Thank You for providing all the armor I need. Amen.*

How Will I Choose Battle?

_____

_____

_____

_____

_____

DAY 48

Choose Rescue

In all their suffering he also suffered, and he personally rescued them. In his love and mercy he redeemed them. He lifted them up and carried them through all the years.

—Isaiah 63:9

I must admit I peeked during the prayer at historical Westminster Abbey. Moments before, Prince Charles had been announced, and the procession of the collegiate body began as we stood to sing "Glorious Things of Thee Are Spoken." I'd hoped Princess Diana was going to be with him. After all, I was wearing my favorite Laura Ashley dress and carrying my Instamatic camera just in case.

It was July 1983, and during this visit to London I was invited to attend with my colleagues a "Service of Thanksgiving for the Life and Work of William Wilberforce." We were remembering before God the 150th anniversary of the death of this great man, reformer, and Christian whose efforts helped rescue countless human souls from slavery.

On February 23, 1807—because of the unwavering efforts of Wilberforce and other committed abolitionists—the British parliament voted to outlaw the slave trade throughout the British Empire. It is said that, amid the hurrahs of Parliament that day, William Wilberforce bowed his head and wept at the culmination of his long battle.

The film, *Amazing Grace*, beautifully depicts the life of Wilberforce, who in his pursuit of rescuing slaves sought to integrate his public life with his faith journey. It took twenty years for legislation to outlaw the slave trade, but then it took another twenty-five years—while Wilberforce struggled with declining health—for the actual emancipation of all slaves in 1833. Methodist minister John Wesley once wrote Wilberforce spurring him on in the midst of this long battle, saying, "Unless God has raised you up for this very thing, you will be worn out by the opposition of men and devils. But if God be for you, who can be against you? Are all of them stronger than God? O be not weary in well doing! Go on, in the name of God and in the power of His might."[1]

Whom are you called to rescue? The answer might even be . . . *yourself*. Perhaps you find yourself enslaved today. Oh, most probably not in real chains, but bound all the same. It might be an addiction or an abusive relationship. Perhaps you're struggling with a destructive habit you simply cannot stop, no matter how hard you try. You too need emancipation, and there is a Rescuer coming your way.

God is our own personal first responder. First responders are continually on the front lines—putting themselves in harm's way in order to rescue victims and often paying the ultimate price for that courageous act. That's why this year I put the new USPS postage stamp honoring first responders on all my Christmas cards.

To remind me (and you) of the choice for rescue.

God has "rescued us from the kingdom of darkness and transferred us into the Kingdom of his dear Son" (Colossians 1:13).

Lord, You are truly my own personal first responder. Will You also stand beside me in the battle against any danger or harmful habit? Will You help me be brave and choose a life of freedom, even when it seems scary? When I need rescue, You show up and provide. Amen.

How Will I Choose Rescue?

_____

_____

_____

_____

_____

_____

_____

_____

_____

_____

_____

_____

_____

_____

_____

_____

_____

_____

_____

_____

_____

_____

_____

Day 49

Choose Rest

God has told his people, "Here is a place of rest; let the weary rest here. This is a place of quiet rest." But they would not listen.

—Isaiah 28:12

A whole week in a cottage by the sea. As a writer, my first thought was I could be quite productive in such an atmosphere.

Or not.

Perhaps instead it was a perfect opportunity to actually Do Nothing. To rest. To walk. To be silent. To listen. To remember. To dream. To create. To be nourished, body and soul.

Victorian art critic John Ruskin once observed:

"There is no music in a rest, but there is the making of music in it." In our whole life-melody the music is broken off here and there by "rests," and we foolishly think we have come to the end of the tune. . . . Not without design does God write the music of our lives. Be it ours to learn the tune and not be dismayed at the "rests." . . . With the eye on him, we shall strike the next note full and clear.[1]

Pauses are essential for those of us who spend our lives creating. And for everyone else too. We are wired with natural rhythms that include times of both music and restful silences.

Are you so full of ideas and plans that you feel as though you may burst? Or are you dry and empty, in dread of facing yet another empty page (or screen)? Either way, it may be time to pull away from it all.

No music for a time. In order to rest.

It helps to unplug from all your devices. Seriously. Then be perfectly quiet. Sit in a comfortable place with your hands open wide. To release and receive.

Release your concerns, anxieties and fears. Ask God to carry them for you or even dispel them altogether. Identify them and then pray:

> *Lord, you know what weighs me down, what hinders my life and my work. And why. I release them now to You, one by one, trusting in Your protection and deliverance. Amen.*

Now release your dreams, hopes and daring ideas to the One who will hone, fashion, and tweak for His best purposes. Identify them and then pray:

> *Lord, I want so much! Keep my vision and goals high and lofty— bold for Your glory. But today, as I name them, I release them back into Your hands, asking You to guide me forward or redirect me as You choose. I want Your will and Your perfect timing. Amen.*

You are now in a position to *receive*. Once again, open your hands and be still. Pray as Samuel did, "Speak, your servant is listening" (1 Samuel 3:10).

Continue in silence. Five minutes may seem like five hours to those of us who love to fill all space with words. But God is so very present in this place as you pray:

> *Lord, I receive from Your love, grace, mercy, hope, joy, forgiveness, wisdom, truth, strength, Holy Spirit power, courage, peace, and a very real sense of Your presence even now as I dwell deeply with You. Reveal to me where to direct my energy and resources*

in my life. Give me grace to face both opened doors and doors slamming shut. Keep me close to You that I might always recognize the Source of all that is worthy to be released to a broken world, through my flawed but willing human vessel. Amen.

No matter how long your restful time apart is, it will be an investment in your life and work, with visible benefits. Maybe not immediately. But cleaning the clutter in your mind and heart makes way for fresh work, a fresh filling. Even our Lord Jesus withdrew to a solitary place for refreshment and renewal—emerging with power.

Will you rest?

Lord, I find it almost impossible to carve out significant time to actually rest. Thank You for wanting me to approach You with open hands—both to release and receive. Help me to schedule a time and place to be restored in Your steadfast strength. Amen.

How Will I Choose Rest?

_____

_____

_____

_____

_____

_____

_____

_____

_____

_____

Choose Nature

For ever since the world was created, people have seen the earth and sky. Through everything God made, they can clearly see his invisible qualities—his eternal power and divine nature. So they have no excuse for not knowing God.

—Romans 1:20

*F*rancis Bacon once said, "God has two textbooks—Scripture and Creation—we would do well to listen to both." And Lilias Trotter "listened" to both. Though born into British privilege and praised as an artist by John Ruskin, Lilias courageously went to North Africa as a single woman, living among Muslim people for four decades and sharing God's love through stories connecting nature and faith.

Every morning she wandered to a quiet place in the woods with her Bible, of which Lilias observed, "It is so delicious on these hot spring mornings, and God rests one through it for the whole day and speaks so through all living things. Day after day something comes afresh."[1]

I have a treasured volume filled with beautiful artwork in which Trotter shares about learning the art of relinquishment—including a lesson she learned from a buttercup:

> The little hands of the calyx clasp tightly in the bud round the beautiful petals; in the young flower their grasp grows more elastic—loosening somewhat in the daytime, but keeping the power of contracting, able to close in again during a rainstorm, or when night comes on. But see the central flower, which has reached its maturity. The calyx hands have unclasped utterly now—they have folded themselves back, past all power of closing again upon the petals, leaving the golden crown free to float away when God's time comes. Have we learned the buttercup's lesson yet? Are our hands off the very blossom of our life? Are all things—even the treasures that He has sanctified—held loosely, ready to be parted with, without a struggle, when He asks for them?[2]

Do you discover life lessons in nature? Perhaps by feeling the wind of His Spirit in the gentle breeze. Or maybe a vigorous hike among solid rock formations reminds you of the strong God who is your fortress.

God uses this beauty to nourish our souls.

> The moon and stars remind us that God's light and love shine to us even in the dark. The Lord is speaking to us and warming us from the heavens . . . Throughout the Bible we read testimony of the Lord communicating to us in the skies, ocean waves, breeze rustling through the trees, fields and flowers, and birds that sing cheerfully. . . . Nature reveals to us God's beauty, glory, power, wisdom, presence, creativity, and, most of all, his loving care.[3]

But we must choose to embrace nature in order to learn from it. Go outside as much as possible. Why not take a walk today in your backyard, through your community, or out into the countryside?

Be sure to notice every small thing—both with your eyes and also with the eyes of your heart. Then do as the psalmist did—respond to the Creator.

O LORD, our Lord, your majestic name fills the earth! Your glory is higher than the heavens. . . . When I look at the night sky and see the work of your fingers—the moon and the stars you set in place—what are mere mortals that you should think about them, human beings that you should care for them?

—Psalm 8:1, 3–4

Nature reveals one of God's most gracious gifts, which our souls cannot live without—beauty. After hiking near his home in Colorado, one man concluded nature is not primarily functional—it is primarily beautiful. He said, "Which is to say, beauty is in and of itself a great and glorious good, something we need in large and daily doses . . . Beauty is the essence of God. The whole world is full of his glory."[4]

> Were the whole realm of nature mine,
> That were a present far too small;
> Love so amazing, so divine,
> Demands my soul, my life, my all.
>
> —Isaac Watts, "When I Survey the Wondrous Cross"

Lord, the world is full of such beautiful creations that I can hardly take it all in. Thank You for knowing we needed stars and flowers, mountains and seas, furry animals and feathered birds. When I spend time with You amongst nature, I feel truly alive. Amen.

How Will I Choose Nature?

_____

_____

_____

_____

_____

_____

_____

_____

_____

_____

_____

_____

_____

_____

_____

_____

_____

_____

_____

_____

Day 51

Choose Humility

So humble yourselves under the mighty power of God, and at the right time he will lift you up in honor.

—1 Peter 5:6

The voice at the other end of the phone was ecstatic, "I love your book— it's so deep, so insightful! I don't understand why you aren't more famous as an author. In fact, you should have been the keynote speaker, not just a seminar leader at that conference. You are an amazing writer! Why haven't I ever heard of your books before?"

I meet so many people when I speak at conferences, and it's always gratifying to hear that my words have been received. Obviously, this unexpected phone call tickled my ears—tempting me to see this young author as my new BFF.

I lapped up the praise, answered her questions, and after hanging up sat very still.

Ashamed that her words echoed my own unspoken thoughts. *Why haven't more people heard of my books? Why am I not the keynote speaker at more events? What real impact has my ministry made throughout the years?*

Writing and speaking encouraging words based on God's Word has been my passion for a lifetime. An obedient response to a definite calling. I walk through the open doors and offer my best, empowered by the Spirit. Always leaving the fruit up to God. And I truly do believe I have been used for kingdom work in people's lives.

Is it so wrong for my heart to wish it were *more?*

While you may not be a writer and speaker, chances are you too occasionally struggle with seeing the fruit of your own labor. We envision our legacy as one thing, only to discover God has a totally different plan. We can still practice humility, not by wanting less but by wanting more for God's glory.

King David thought his life's crowning glory would be to build the Temple. He cast the vision, created the blueprint, gathered equipment, assembled a skilled team, and laid the foundation. How he must have reeled from the news that God had instead chosen his son, Solomon, to complete it. All that work—all that wisdom and knowledge of a lifetime—and someone else would be the one to yield the glory!

Solomon quickly affirmed his father's role by reminding the people the Lord had said to David, "You wanted to build the Temple to honor my name. Your intention is good" (2 Chronicles 6:8).

David's dream was a good thing. Releasing it to another (as God instructed) was even better.

I was reminded of the words my friend Christin Ditchfield shared—words that penetrated my heart deeply, causing me to weep silently: "Some of us are called to prepare the way, to blaze the trail for those who come after us and whose progress will far exceed our own. They will stand on our shoulders, just as we have stood on the shoulders of those who came before us."

Is it enough to be the trailblazer? To be the one who invests in those who will far surpass my own work? To relinquish the accolades to another?

Absolutely. Of course. In fact, this *is* my passion—equipping and empowering others to go forth. Beyond me.

> True humility is demonstrated when you have something and give it up voluntarily. It is also shown by not praising yourself even if you deserve praise (Proverbs 27:2), by serving the undeserving (Matthew 20:26), by not choosing the place of prominence (Luke 14:10), by letting God vindicate you (Luke 12), and by submission to elders (1 Peter 5:5–6).
> —Michael M. Smith, *Becoming More Like Jesus*[1]

Can you also choose the path of humility, whatever that means in your life?

Pray with me the closing words of a favorite hundred-year-old prayer, "Litany of Humility":

That others may be loved more than I,
Jesus, grant me the grace to desire it.
That others may be esteemed more than I,
Jesus, grant me the grace to desire it.
That in the opinion of the world, others may increase and I may decrease,
Jesus, grant me the grace to desire it. . . .
That others may become holier than I, provided that I may become as holy as I should,
Jesus, grant me the grace to desire it.

—Cardinal Raphael Merry del Val

Lord, You alone know the deep secrets and desires of my heart. Will You help conform them to Your will and not my own? May I learn to the great joy and fulfillment in lifting others for Your glory. Amen.

How Will I Choose Humility?

_____

_____

_____

_____

_____

_____

_____

Day 52

Choose Compassion

The LORD is gracious and righteous; our God is full of compassion.

—Psalm 116:5 NIV

*Y*et again I found myself quietly weeping.

The evening news brought such violence and tragedy my heart and soul could hardly absorb the reality of it all. I wondered how long before the shock would end and my emotions would shut down completely from such things.

On the 311th day of the year 2018, a mass shooting in Thousand Oaks, California, took the lives of thirteen people, including the gunman. It was the 307th mass shooting for that year. *That's almost one violent mass shooting per day.* No wonder our coping mechanism is often to just numb our feelings.

Compassion fatigue has gripped our world. When there is too much to handle, we just don't.

And yet God has called us to be people of compassion. This biblical word is derived from two Latin words that together mean "to suffer with." Compassionate people are those who suffer alongside someone else in their pain and tragedy.

Compassion asks us to go where it hurts, to enter into places of pain, to share in brokenness, fear, confusion, and anguish. Compassion challenges us to cry out with those in misery, to mourn with those who are lonely, to weep with those in tears. Compassion requires us to be weak with the weak, vulnerable with the vulnerable, and powerless with the powerless. Compassion means full immersion in the condition of being human. When we look at compassion this way, it becomes clear that something more is involved than a general kindness or tenderheartedness. —Henri Nouwen, Donald McNeill, and Douglas Morrison, *Compassion: A Reflection on the Christian Life*[1]

What hinders you from living out compassion in your daily life? Often our lack of intention is the cause of not living with compassion; other times it can be something deeper. PTSD (post-traumatic stress disorder) is no longer only associated with military veterans. And STS (secondary traumatic stress) is gaining ground. STS is a vicarious traumatization that occurs when there is a cumulative level of trauma—such as horrific news over and over again. First responders and people in helping professions are also susceptible to this.

One psychologist offers some suggestions for dealing with compassion fatigue:

- Limit the amount of daily news you watch or read about
- Try to come to terms with the fact that pain and suffering are realities of life over which we have little to no control
- Be grateful for what is good in your life and in the world
- Try to find some meaning in the suffering you see
- If you must blame something, blame the situation, not the person
- Show compassion to yourself by being kind, soothing, and comforting to yourself
- By being aware of the warning signs of compassion fatigue, you can prevent it and continue to do what you do best—change lives for the better with one act of kindness at a time. —Dr. Sherrie Bourg Carter, "Are You Suffering from Compassion Fatigue?"[2]

I would add at least one more thing to that list: Remember God is sovereign—"gracious and righteous . . . full of compassion."

Our Lord Jesus saw and experienced every kind of pain imaginable, and yet He offered compassion to all He encountered. We continually read in the Gospels, "he had compassion on them" (such as in Matthew 9:36 and 14:14). And the Apostle Paul exhorted believers, "Therefore, as God's chosen people, holy and dearly loved, clothe yourselves with compassion" (Colossians 3:12 NIV).

It is our joy and privilege to choose to put on compassion today and every day. If we don't, who will?

> *Lord, my heart hurts to see others who are suffering—those whose homes have been destroyed or families separated. Children starving from hunger and parents escaping bombs. Keep me sensitive and sorrowful so I might reach out and help in some small way. Amen.*

How Will I Choose Compassion?

_____

_____

_____

_____

_____

_____

_____

_____

_____

_____

Day 53

Choose Life

I came so they can have real and eternal life, more and better life than they ever dreamed of.

—John 10:10 *The Message*

Do any human beings ever realize life while they live it—every, every minute?" asked Emily in Thornton Wilder's play *Our Town*.

Emily, who has died, has the opportunity to visit her life for one day. As she observes everyone just going through the motions, she finally recognizes life for the treasure that it was—one she can never have again. "Let's really look at one another!" she entreats people who cannot see or hear her. "I can't go on. It goes so fast. We don't have time to look at one another. I didn't realize. So all that was going on in life and we never noticed!"[1]

Are you in danger of not noticing your own precious life?

With heightened technology and our culture's fast pace, many of us fail to look one another in the eye and enjoy the moments. To truly live our lives to the fullest. Because the days may seem long, but the years are indeed short! Ask any mama.

So why don't we recognize life for the treasure it is?

C. S. Lewis observed that too often our desires are not too strong but rather too weak when he said, "We are half-hearted creatures, fooling about with drink and sex and ambition when infinite joy is offered us, like an ignorant child who wants to go on making mud pies in a slum because he cannot imagine what is meant by the offer of a holiday at the sea. We are far too easily pleased."[2]

Friend, if you do what you've always done, you'll have what you've always had. But if you want what you've never had, you must do what you've never done. In her poem "The Summer Day," Mary Oliver posed the question, "What is it you plan to do with your one wild and precious life?" and it is one we all must answer.

God's Word has much to say about living fully through Christ:

In him was life, and that life was the light of all mankind.

—John 1:4 NIV

Stand firm, and you will win life.

—Luke 21:19 NIV

And here I am, standing right before you, and you aren't willing to receive from me the life you say you want.

—John 5:40 *The Message*

I tell you the truth, anyone who believes has eternal life. Yes, I am the bread of life!

—John 6:47–48

I have come that they may have life, and have it to the full.

—John 10:10 NIV

You have shown me the way of life, and you will fill me with the joy of your presence.

—Acts 2:28

I urge you to live a life worthy of the calling you have received.

—Ephesians 4:1 NIV

By his divine power, God has given us everything we need for living a godly life.

—2 Peter 1:3

What are you waiting for in order to truly live: That last child to leave the home (or even just go to kindergarten)? For things at work to finally slow down (or for retirement)? When you finally get your weight/finances/schedule under control?

Blaise Pascal observed, "We are never living, but hoping to live; and whilst we are always preparing to be happy, it is certain, we never shall be so."[3]

Choose life. Today.

Lord, what am I waiting for in order to fully pursue a life with purpose and passion? Help me realize that time is moving on and embrace each opportunity as a chance for learning, serving, growing, and giving. Thank You for my life today. Amen.

How Will I Choose Life?

_____

_____

_____

_____

_____

_____

_____

_____

_____

_____

_____

_____

_____

Choose Worship

All together now—applause for God! Sing songs to the tune of his glory, set glory to the rhythms of his praise. Say of God, "We've never seen anything like him!" When your enemies see you in action, they slink off like scolded dogs. The whole earth falls to its knees—it worships you, sings to you, can't stop enjoying your name and fame.

—Psalm 66:1–4 *The Message*

The smells were different. The sights were different. The music was different. And even some of the words were different.

But it was the same God.

I recently attended worship in a Christian church culturally not my own. In such a situation, often the *differences* are what initially bombard the senses. Incense and icons. Chanting of unfamiliar music. Robes of gold and an exquisitely painted dome.

I was reminded of "different" services I'd experienced in other lands—preaching from a flat-bed truck in Malawi, on the beach in Thailand, gathering in a dark hut in northern Kenya, and sitting in the back pew of a Mediterranean camp church where it was literally "all Greek to me." Here in the States, I've worshipped in gymnasiums, cathedrals, tents, stone chapels, and, yes, even a Kentucky country church with snake-handlers!

Yet in all these places the *same* Jesus Christ was lifted up and worshipped. Personally, I would rather embrace my common beliefs with other

Christians rather than focus on our differences. True, there *are* distinct differences. But we have the same Scripture and the same Lord and Savior. "There is one God and one Mediator who can reconcile God and humanity—the man Christ Jesus" (1 Timothy 2:5).

Why not build bridges instead of walls?

That said, I do acknowledge different can often be uncomfortable. It is human nature to seek the solace of the familiar. And far too often our insecurities prompt criticism —"Why do they sing *choruses* instead of hymns?" or "Why do they sing *hymns* instead of choruses?" or "Why do they *chant* instead of singing hymns and choruses?"

Do you think God is actually big enough to receive our praise and worship in a whole world full of creative ways? Do you think perhaps our prayers reach God's ears whether they are totally spontaneous or whether we pray from the heart the words of an ancient prayer? I do both. And I assure you God hears.

God knows the heart of the worshipper. He knows whether or not we are focused on Him, committed to Him, believing the words we sing and recite. Somehow I don't think God cares as much about the *form* as we do. He cares that we trust and believe and hope and worship.

> May God, who gives this patience and encouragement, help you live in complete harmony with each other, as is fitting for followers of Christ Jesus. Then all of you can join together with one voice, giving praise and glory to God, the Father of our Lord Jesus Christ. Therefore, accept each other just as Christ has accepted you so that God will be given glory.
>
> —Romans 15:5–7

And whether God's people gather in an urban storefront or an underground cellar, or, yes, even an ornate sanctuary, He is among us.

Frankly, I'm not crazy about religious labels. I am a Christ follower. That's all that really matters. For the past twenty-eight years, my home of worship is the oldest church in the state of Connecticut. Gathered in 1635, our sanctuary is called The Meetinghouse, and we worship in a Puritan white simple edifice with doored pews and a high pulpit with absolutely no decoration whatsoever! In fact, it remains the same as when George Washington and Jonathan Edwards worshipped here hundreds of years ago.

And it couldn't be a more different atmosphere from the church mentioned in my opening. Yet here I find God. As do hundreds who attend our Sunday services. Do you find God where you worship? Isn't that what truly matters?

After all, it's not about me. It's about Him.

How will you choose to worship today? With great joy? In reverence? Just open your Bible to the Book of Psalms.

> Come, let us worship and bow down. Let us kneel before the LORD our maker.
>
> —Psalm 95:6

> Enter his gates with thanksgiving; go into his courts with praise. Give thanks to him and praise his name. For the LORD is good. His unfailing love continues forever, and his faithfulness continues to each generation.
>
> —Psalm 100:4–5

As Timothy Keller proclaims in *The Songs of Jesus,* "Glorious worship is exuberant, never halfhearted. It is attractive, not off-putting. It is awesome, never sentimental. It is brilliant, not careless. It points to God, not to the speakers."[1]

Is it time to point to God?

Lord, You are indeed worthy of all my worship and praise. If I sang and danced and shouted hallelujah for a lifetime, it would never be enough. So instead I will recount Your many blessings and gifts and answers to prayer. I love You with all I am and all I have. Amen.

How Will I Choose Worship?

_____

_____

_____

_____

_____

_____

_____

_____

_____

_____

_____

_____

_____

_____

_____

_____

_____

_____

_____

_____

_____

_____

_____

_____

_____

Choose Questions

When Jesus saw him lying there and learned that he had been in this condition for a long time, he asked him, "Do you want to get well?"

—John 5:6 NIV

"Who is your favorite literary character and why?" was the question that opened our online study, a weekly gathering of ten women from all over the country.

What ensued was a lively discussion of our childhood heroines, including insight into how those characters may have helped shape the course of our lives. Though we had known each other for many years, our answers were surprising and provocative.

That discussion question comes from a new Dutch parlor game called *Vertellis*. This name is derived from two Dutch words, *vertel eens,* which loosely translate to "tell me more." The game is not just about answering questions but also about fully engaging. The creators' mission is to bring people together at a time when we seem to be distracted by technology and ambition. The *Vertellis* team hopes to make a positive impact in the world by facilitating beautiful conversations and stimulate time offline.

Questions have a way of doing that—good questions get right to the core. And in answering them we often learn about ourselves.

Here are just a few examples of when Jesus used questions to help prompt people to identify their feelings, their needs, and what to do next.

"Do you want to get well?" John 5:6 NIV

(to the man who had lain by the pool of Bethesda for thirty-eight years, hoping to be healed)

"Who do you say I am?" Matthew 16:15

(to Peter who answered "You are the Messiah" in verse 16; then Jesus told Peter He would build the church on this rock)

"Who touched me?" Luke 8:45

(in the crowd when the woman with an issue of blood reached out for healing and restoration)

"What do you want me to do for you?" Mark 10:51

(asking Bartimaeus, who responded, "I want to see," and immediately his sight was restored)

"Do you love me?" John 21:15

(on the shore after the Resurrection, Jesus gave Peter three times to answer and affirm his love and commitment to "feed my sheep")

"Which of these three would you say was a neighbor?" Luke 10:36

(after telling the parable of the man put upon by thieves and showing that only the Samaritan helped him)

Are there ways you could use questions to improve your own relationships?

For instance, when a child first arrives home from school, don't just ask, "How was school?" or you run the risk of hearing a short, nonspecific answer like, "Fine." Instead, ask something that stimulates conversation, possibly revealing more about your child's day. Questions such as:

What made you smile today?

Did you hear anything that surprised you?

Who did you play with/talk to at recess?

What new word did you learn?

How were you helpful today?

Questions can also be a vehicle for our own spiritual growth. Do not hesitate to voice to God those things with which you are struggling. Look for answers in His Word and through godly counsel. As writer Stephen Mattson reminds us, "We're continually faced with questions that challenge our belief systems. This isn't a bad thing, and much of Jesus's ministry revolved around asking questions. In the end, thoughtfully examining our faith promotes a spirituality that is healthy, honest, genuine, and mature."[1]

A treasured gift I received recently is the devotional book, *Sacred Questions*, in which the author's own spiritual journey began with questions—bringing them to God, not just to receive answers but to also be changed. In the process, God used that questioning to allow her to know Him and herself even better, to break patterns of sin, grow in forgiveness and love, and join his work in the world.

> Asking sacred questions opens a holy dialogue with the loving, ever-present God who is at once holding all things together and dwelling within us. Instead of doing all the talking, we learn how to listen for what God is saying. We all long for space to hear him, to allow ourselves to receive his love, and yet we often either fail to make the time or are unsure how to do it (and maybe a little of both). —Kellye Fabian, *Sacred Questions: A Transformative Journey through the Bible*[2]

So go ahead, ask away. God loves to answer our questions.

Lord, sometimes I feel guilty when I question something most Christians simply take for granted. Thank You for allowing me to freely search and learn—about You, about faith, and even about my place in the world. Your answers always satisfy. Amen.

How Will I Choose Questions?

DAY 56

Choose Shelter

God is our shelter and strength, always ready to help in times of trouble.

—Psalm 46:1

I wrestled with the small tarp, trying in vain to cover both myself and my sleeping bag against the cold mountain air.

This was my only shelter on the two-day solo hike of our seminary wilderness class. But it did absolutely nothing to make me feel safe or secure—because of potential bears, we had no food, just a whistle to blow in case of emergency. Needless to say, I did not sleep at all in the pitch-black darkness. In fact, I lay there all night with the whistle in my mouth. Just in case.

It's no surprise that Maslow's hierarchy of needs begins with survival—humans cannot live without food, water, shelter, sleep, and oxygen. As those are met, other needs emerge throughout the hierarchy: physical safety, love and belonging, self-esteem, and self-fulfillment.

All over our world today there are countless people in search of shelter. Homeless, they long for home. Refugees, they only desire refuge. Fearful, they seek sanctuary—a safe place.

And we simply have no idea. Most who are reading this book are fortunate enough to close a door and crawl into a bed each night. With no need of a whistle in our mouths.

How can we *find* shelter? How can we actually *be* shelter to someone else? There is really only one answer—God.

In today's text the original Hebrew word used for shelter was *machaseh*. This word is also related to the Hebrew word *chasah*, which we translate to take refuge and trust. Combined together, those words—trust, refuge, shelter—may seem hard to come by these days.

Only God "is our shelter and strength." He is the one who is "always ready," the one to "help in times of trouble."

When we find shelter in God—and not just in a place or person—we are trusting One who will not change. Unlike our physical places of shelter, which constantly change. We might live in an apartment, a cottage, or a dormitory depending on our needs and life situation at the time. But what a difference occurs when we actually invite God into our place of shelter. Whatever corner we occupy can become a place of beauty and serenity. Welcoming. Simplicity, color, light, plants, and a generous spirit bring a sort of coziness that beckons others to settle in safely. The Danish people call this *hygge*.

Prounounced "hoo-guh," hygge refers to an atmosphere that evokes feelings of comfort, coziness, and contentment. It is related to both Norwegian and English words that mean to hug. No wonder so many are embracing hygge today—we want to be hugged! Hygge encourages its practitioners to shelter, cluster, and enclose.

Experts cast hygge "as a state of mindfulness: how to make essential and mundane tasks dignified, joyful, and beautiful, how to live a life connected with loved ones" and focus "on the concept's philosophical and spiritual underpinnings rather than its quirky objects. . . . Many households in Denmark still have a copy of a folk songbook that they sing from to affirm the ideas of simplicity, cheerfulness, reciprocity, community, and belonging."[1]

Does your home offer that elusive feeling of shelter and sanctuary to the ones living and visiting there?

The late Walter and Ingrid Trobisch spent much of the twentieth century helping young people embrace God's shelter. After becoming widowed, Ingrid named her new home *Haus Geborgenheit,* which is German for "place of steadfast shelter." I am grateful to her for teaching me when I was a young wife and mother about the importance of creating a sense of emotional safety in a home.

> Perhaps the greater the Shelter or family feeling children experience growing up, the more they'll miss it when it's not there, and as adults, the harder they'll work to create it around their own hearth. Those who have never had it may crave it more deeply yet. I see many people hungry for this. . . . By allowing vulnerable experiences in quiet and rest, you become a person who makes every context a safe place. Your life becomes Shelter—whether giving a good night kiss to a child or listening to the secret dreams of a spouse. —Ingrid Trobisch, *Keeper of the Springs*[2]

My great joy was the day—the only day out of the entire year my whole family gathered together from afar—we ushered in a new year at our home, named Sunnyside Cottage. I'm so grateful all my children still enjoy coming home.

May your life become shelter.

Lord, it's not just enough to have a roof over my head; I also long for true shelter that provides both warmth and welcome. I'm grateful You provide that, no matter where I go. Show me how to be the kind of presence that brings trust and security to others. Amen.

How Will I Choose Shelter?

_____
_____
_____
_____
_____
_____
_____
_____
_____
_____
_____
_____
_____
_____
_____
_____
_____
_____
_____
_____
_____
_____
_____

Choose Significance

> But I also want you to think about how this keeps your significance from getting blown up into self-importance. For no matter how significant you are, it is only because of what you are a part of.
>
> —1 Corinthians 12:19 *The Message*

When I was a little girl, I wanted to be famous.

A child movie star, in fact. More precisely, I wanted to be Hayley Mills. For those of you too young to remember, she was the Disney darling who starred in many films, such as *Pollyanna* and *The Parent Trap*. I was the original fan girl—to the extent that for at least a year I styled my hair the same as Hayley did in *Pollyanna* and even wore drop-waisted dresses with black stockings. Oh yeah.

One day I wrote a letter to Hayley Mills. I decided if I couldn't be *her*, I could at least get advice for my own trajectory into stardom. I began (as any good fan letter does) with a full-on gush—"You are my favorite movie star!" and continued on to the meat of the matter . . . "How do you become a movie star? I want to be one while I am a child."

Then I listed a few credentials to impress her: "When our school has plays or recitals I always join in. I'm not scared to go on stage at all. I've been the leading part in most of my plays. I'm not bragging, I just want some tips on acting. I can sing, act, and dance. I've been taking music for two years."

Wow. Two whole years of music lessons! Now that I had her attention and formed a kindred spirit bond, I continued . . . "You've sent lots of my friends postcards and pictures. But I want and need a long letter from you."

There you go. Surely Hayley would begin to open doors to my new career! What with all that talent and experience I might even give her some competition for the next Disney movie. Nonetheless, my insecurity resurrected as I prepared my closing, and I was not too proud to beg. "Please, I want to be a young movie star so bad. Please write me a long letter. Your best of friends, Cindy Secrest, 10 years old."

Hayley never wrote me back. But since I have in my hand a faded and wrinkled piece of paper that looks strangely like the original letter I asked my parents to mail, I can only surmise that, due to not knowing her address, they tucked it into a file somewhere only to be retrieved five decades later.

I don't blame Mama and Daddy for singlehandedly putting the kibosh on all my child-acting dreams. Because life has a way of restoring balance.

The month I turned fourteen, Hayley Mills and I sailed the Atlantic together on the *Queen Elizabeth I* ocean liner. Well, not actually *together*, but I did get to meet her on deck for a chat and a photo. My family was returning from a European holiday and were fortunate enough to be on the very last cross-Atlantic voyage of that historic ship. As a teenager coming home from London's Carnaby Street and Abbey Road, full of Twiggy and the Beatles, I was way too cool to ask her for acting tips.

It's just as well. God did not call me to stardom—He called me to significance.

He had other plans for that bold, outspoken character who was never afraid to go on stage. So I kept pursuing dreams. I tried on a few hats—some were a terrible fit and others stayed on for a while.

And the whole time I was dancing through life *I wrote things down.* On lined paper. In journals. On my large print typewriter. Using a flair pen. In letters and cards. And eventually on my new personal computer! I also found myself on stage occasionally and discovered that when Holy Spirit power poured through me, I was in a personal sweet spot—sharing stories and words of encouragement.

What is your own sweet spot of significance?

Living significant does not mean we are famous, just that we are filled with and pouring out whatever helps change lives—for the better. Significance has its own luster, and to those who matter, it shines brighter than stars.

What sage advice would I give that ten-year-old Cindy Secrest?

- Keep writing letters to anyone you wish—always begin with praise, and don't hesitate to ask questions. What's the worst that can happen? If they say *no*, move on. But realize that some letters are best never mailed.

- Always ask yourself the motivation for why you want to do something that commands attention. You might need to reconsider. If you aren't afraid of a stage microphone, that doesn't make you brave— it's probably just the way God wired you.

- Be willing to adjust your goals and dreams as experience, mistakes, victories, and critique help show you who you truly are. And keep singing.

When you look back over a lifetime, *thank God for the unique way He created you and seek with all your heart to honor Him in all your pursuits.* Significantly. If that happens to include music, stories, and the occasional stage, then honey, give it all you've got!

> *Lord, I've always wanted to make a difference in the world—for my life to count. Sometimes I've mixed that up with "success," but now I realize what I really seek is to have a life of "significance." Guide me to invest in that which will matter for eternity. Amen.*

How Will I Choose Significance?

_____

_____

_____

_____

_____

_____

_____

_____

_____

_____

_____

_____

_____

_____

_____

_____

_____

_____

_____

_____

_____

_____

_____

_____

_____

Day 58

Choose Legacy

"You intended to harm me, but God intended it all for good. He brought me to this position so I could save the lives of many people." . . . So he reassured them by speaking kindly to them.

—Genesis 50:20–21

Joseph—one of the Bible's great heroes—grew up in a dysfunctional family.

Joseph's father Jacob greatly deceived his own father Isaac and stole his brother Esau's birthright. Then Jacob's own future father-in-law Laban deceived Jacob by marrying him off not to his intended bride Rachel but to her sister Leah before finally giving the desired Rachel in marriage. Not only that, but Joseph had many stepbrothers from his father's four wives. He and his little brother Benjamin were the only ones born to his late mother Rachel. And Jacob loved them more.

Because Joseph was bright, handsome, and given to interpreting dreams, he acted quite proudly in flaunting his gift from Dad—the multicolored coat. He also freely boasted about his dream in which all his brothers were bowing down to him. None of this won him any popularity contests, and he became doomed by circumstances beyond his control.

His brothers sold him into slavery, pretended he was killed, and returned his multicolored coat—which the brothers had dipped into goat's blood—to a distraught father.

Even as this drama was unfolding, Joseph held tightly to the good part of his family heritage—a people who trusted God, however imperfectly. Even when he was falsely accused of sexual impropriety with Potiphar's wife and thrown into prison, Scripture records, "The LORD was with him" (Genesis 39:23). Later, when Pharaoh was looking for a man to help lead his people, he noticed Joseph was "filled with the spirit of God" (Genesis 41:38).

Joseph had languished in prison for years, but as he interpreted Pharaoh's dream about the upcoming famine, he was entrusted to lead the country through this crisis as Pharaoh declared, "You will be in charge of my court, and all my people will take orders from you. Only I, sitting on my throne, will have a rank higher than yours" (v. 40).

What a roller coaster life Joseph experienced—ups and downs aplenty. Perhaps in your own family there have been both positive and negative experiences. Remember, nothing is wasted on your journey. Joseph's ultimate role was to be a courageous leader and help save people, but God used Joseph's time in prison to prepare him inwardly for what he would need—trust, strength, perseverance, and mercy.

For the next fourteen years Joseph moved on with his life—he married, had children, and probably thought often about a potential encounter with his estranged brothers. On the day they arrived to beg for food to this unrecognizable prime minister, Joseph was so overcome he had to leave the room and weep. His childhood dreams had literally come true as they knelt before him! And yes, Joseph did use a bit of trickery in order to test their hearts and have them bring back his brother Benjamin. But he eventually revealed himself to his brothers, which scared them to death.

Would he now get revenge? Or was it finally time to stop the legacy of lies and jealousy, deceit and violence?

Our verse today reveals clearly that Joseph made a choice to forgive his brothers and to help write a new family saga. He brought his elderly father and his brothers' families into a new land and continued to bless them, even after his father Jacob died. What a testimony of how God can take the evil works of people (even family members) and use them to bring about the story He wants to write in the life of a person willing to be used of Him.

No matter what happened in your family of origin, you can forge a new path and leave a new legacy.

> Who will teach the next generation how to heal? How to hope? How to love? How to be a woman of integrity and faith? We will. And we will do it not only with words but with the very essence of who we have become as God's daughters. . . . Healing isn't just for us. It's for those who follow us. Do others see the love of God in us? Have they experienced Him in our choices to love, accept, and forgive? How we love, how we hope, and how we live our lives are the very things we pass on. —Debbie Alsdorf, *It's Momplicated: Hope and Healing for Imperfect Daughters of Imperfect Mothers*[1]

Lord, I can't help but wonder what I will leave behind after I'm gone. I want others to remember my faithfulness and kindness, not all those times I got it wrong. Help me freely offer reconciliation, forgiveness, and encouragement to all, beginning with my family. Amen.

How Will I Choose Legacy?

_____

_____

_____

_____

_____

_____

Choose Discernment

Let the wise listen and add to their learning, and let the discerning get guidance.

—Proverbs 1:5 NIV

*M*ine was the last plane out before the snowstorm hit New England. I was escaping to a warmer clime for a "desperate respite" thanks to the gracious hospitality of friends.

Long days beside the wind and waves quieted my soul (and my weary, throbbing brain) to a place where I could actually hear God's whisper.

I want to hear this voice. And be sure the words are from God and not me.

> The voice of the Spirit is as gentle as a zephyr, so gentle that unless you are living in perfect communion with God, you never hear it. The checks of the Spirit come in the most extraordinarily gentle ways, and if you are not sensitive enough to detect His voice you will quench it, and your personal spiritual life will be impaired. His checks always come as a still small voice, so small that no one but the saint notices them.
> —Oswald Chambers, *My Utmost for His Highest*[1]

For many of us it takes time and deliberate withdrawal to come to a place where we can fully receive God's marching orders for a new season. And so holy men retreat to the desert. And I go to the beach. In the dead of winter.

A month when the wind is fierce and loud, the waves pound upon the shore as though to rhythmically remind me of my Creator's power and presence.

It's not terribly peaceful but in fact more *stirring*. Reflecting my own inner stirrings and desire to be released with fresh power of my own for whatever may be ahead.

At its core my identity has always been *God's beloved*. But I believe it is time to add to that—*seasoned mentor*.

Because this is the new mandate God's whisper revealed so clearly when I was finally able to settle down long enough to truly listen and receive:

My beloved Lucinda,

This is a season to share the story of what you have learned through My presence, power, and provision. How letting go of grasping helped you receive the gift of grace; how healing in your brokenness refined your view of scars as beautiful. How filling up with more of Me allowed you to freely pour out for others in strength and service.

Tell them. Show them. Point out that there are always more options than the ones loudly appearing front and center. That one must go deeper—sometimes bending quite low—to discover My best. Warn them that it will take great courage and faith to make wise choices, so they must live boldly. With Me.

Stand steadfast in your belief that what you have based your entire life on is true. Essential. Learn how to live simply. Focus. Persevere, even if you are ignored as irrelevant.

You have already learned the hard lesson of dwelling deep; now do it. Begin at home. Then allow Me to open other doors.

Fling grace widely, everywhere you go—just as Miss Rumphius did with lupine seeds in Barbara Cooney's storybook! (And yes, some folks called her a crazy old lady.)

This will be a sweet season. Don't worry about legacy, just love. Serve.

I am here. Always have been. Always will be. Because you are Mine. Beloved.

Love,
Your Heavenly Father

I carefully pack up those precious words for the trip back to my real life. To the noisy and needy. The immediate and important. The clutter and the cold. But I am fortified and steadfast. And not alone.

In listening to God's whisper, I discerned several intimate messages I hold close in my heart. But especially the one that confirmed why I am here for others: *helping you choose a life of serenity and strength.*

What will He whisper to you?

Lord, I talk way more than I listen, but I want to change that. Thank You for calling me into the sweet place of focusing on Your voice, Your message, and Your love. Once I've heard, please help me to clearly discern and respond in faith. Amen.

How Will I Choose Discernment?

_____

_____

_____

_____

_____

_____

_____

Day 60

Choose Steadfast

> Therefore, my beloved, be steadfast, immovable, always excelling in the work of the Lord, because you know that in the Lord your labor is not in vain.
>
> —1 Corinthians 15:58 NRSV

*F*or some time now, I have enjoyed the discipline of choosing a word for the year—one word to focus on and study in Scripture, a word I believe God will weave into my own life as the days unfold. There's nothing magical about how each word is decided upon—somehow through prayer and circumstances, it simply becomes clear to me in late December or early January.

So when I realized what my word for last year was going to be, I promptly told God I didn't really want that word. *Steadfast.* It hinted of struggle and perhaps a strength I wasn't sure I had.

But in obedience, I began to embrace two obvious facets of steadfast:

Reveling in God's Steadfast Love: "The steadfast love of the LORD never ceases; his mercies never come to an end" (Lamentations 3:22 ESV). In this verse, the Hebrew word *hesed Adonai* is translated into "God's steadfast love."

Seeking to Become More Steadfast: "Let steadfastness have its full effect, that you may be perfect and complete, lacking in nothing" (James 1:4 ESV). In this verse, the Greek word *hupomone* is translated into "steadfastness."

God's steadfast love for me is evident at the start of today's verse as we are addressed as "my beloved." That is the starting place for any situation that calls for strength and stamina—approaching it from a confident position of *beloved.* When we know who we are, we can live loved.

But Paul's exhortation in the 1 Corinthians 15 text breaks down into three specific mandates to me:

Be **Steadfast:** Feet planted firmly, no wavering and fickle folly— "immovable." Know what you believe and *live it.* Discover what God is calling you to and *do it.*

Be **Superb:** Are you "always excelling in the work of the Lord"? No shortcuts just to get by. Fully soaked in the moment, wringing every single life lesson from the challenge. Do *more* than is called for. As the sign on my desk says, "Be kinder than necessary."

Be **Significant:** Your steadfastness today has ramifications for a future you will never see—"in the Lord your labor is not in vain." What we do matters. How we live can literally change the world. Moving forward is a choice you will never regret. Because significance is far more important than success.

As this year began, I had no idea I would watch my husband go through brain surgery and a slight stroke. I could not have anticipated my new grandson struggling for life during a week in intensive care. Or my ninety-one-year-old mama breaking her back and her leg at the same time during a bad episode of the flu. When I didn't know what to do and couldn't find the caregiving strength to maintain order, a cheerful spirit, spiritual confidence, and divine wisdom in all that was swirling around me, God showed up.

I was never standing alone and neither are you.

My year of seeking steadfast was also filled with much more mundane challenges of complicated relationships, financial juggling, discipline fails, professional discouragement, and professional affirmation. The truth is we have countless opportunities to choose steadfast. Every. Single. Day.

Will you dig deep and summon up every single ounce of strength and courage to persevere? To launch forward into the life God has planned for you—full of drama and discouragement, daring and delight?

My favorite visual of what steadfast looks like comes from a scene in the film *The Lord of the Rings: The Return of the King* based on J. R. R. Tolkien's book. The returning king Aragorn (played by actor Viggo Mortensen) is on his horse, rallying the riders behind him against the forces of evil. His men are greatly outnumbered by the evil Orcs, and the battle seems hopeless. But when Aragorn speaks, he *becomes* the king—the role he was called to play in this epic:

> I see in your eyes the same fear that would take the heart of me . . . A day may come when the courage of men fails, when we forsake our friends and break all bonds of fellowship. . . . But it is not *this* day! This day we fight! By all that you hold dear on this good earth—I bid you stand! —*The Lord of the Rings: the Return of the King*, screenplay by Fran Walsh and directed by Peter Jackson

And with those words he leads the charge against the enemy, with ultimate triumph.

I know life is difficult.

We are constantly surrounded by people and circumstances that leave deep soul wounds and render us battle weary. And sometimes we feel we simply cannot take it any longer.

One day our courage *may* fail. One day we *may* forsake friends, fellowship, and faith. But, dear sister, may it not be *this* day!

This day may we "let steadfastness have its full effect." May we live well with integrity and honor and endurance because our story matters to God and to those who come behind us.

This is perhaps one of our most important choices of all.

Lord, thank You for teaching me what it takes to stand with perseverance with You always by my side. Help me in the days ahead to make wise choices that can transform my life into one of strength, serenity, and steadfast faithfulness. I am so grateful for these lessons. Amen.

How Will I Choose Steadfast?

_____

_____

_____

_____

_____

_____

_____

_____

_____

_____

_____

_____

_____

_____

_____

_____

Gratitudes

*T*hanks to *you* for embarking on this courageous sixty-day journey through God's Word with me—I trust it has been a catalyst for discerning what matters most and pursuing your own life-giving choices. While your investment in reading this book thrills me as the author, what is far more important is that your efforts at seeking and growth honor God.

I am humbled and grateful to each person who takes time to read my scribbled words or listen to my spoken words. I take my calling seriously— myself, not so much. You honor me.

I am grateful to Ramona Richards, Tina Atchenson, Meredith Dunn, Reagan Jackson, Charissa Newell, the wonderful sales team, and the entire staff at New Hope Publishers and Iron Stream Media for clearly seeing the vision and importance of the message of *Life-Giving Choices.* An entire community has partnered to produce the volume in your hands today.

Thank you to so many who daily encourage and pray for me. As I shared in this book, connections and friendship are vitally important. I send special thanks to the amazing women in these treasured communities of which I am a part: SpaSisters (you know who you are); Redbud Writers Guild; my *reNEW—retreat for New England Writing and Speaking* community (Rachel and others); Daybreak Prayer Group (Karen, Judy, and Jessica); Growth Group (Kathy, Helga, Vickie, and Colette); Writers Group (Tessa and Lauren); and my Advanced Writers and Speakers Association (AWSA) colleagues.

A big shout-out to all the strong women in my family who still claim me! Gratitudes to all kinfolk of the clans McDowell, Secrest, Hasty, van Seventer, Karpoff, and Stallings. A special thanks to my two grandmothers: Minlu

Chastain Hasty and Catharine Evelyn Secrest. Both of these women, born at the cusp of the twentieth century, made courageous choices their whole lives and set a great example for me. Now that I'm a granny, I appreciate them even more.

Special thank you to Mama—Sarah Hasty Secrest—to whom I dedicate this book. She not only gave me life, love, and daily prayers, but she was also the very first to guide me in making wise life choices. I would not be who I am today without her strength, soul, and sacrifice. Also my sisters Cathy and Susan and my sisters-of-the-heart Maggie and Claire—you are always there for me. Thank you for your unconditional acceptance of this flawed human who loves you all.

As always, my immediate family is my greatest source of encouragement and joy. Gigantic gratitudes to my husband Mike who has steadfastly stood by me for thirty-five years, and to Justin, Tim, Fiona, Tim K, Darlin' Girl, Little Prince, Baby Brother, Maggie, Stephen, and Sweet T. Each of you represents the best choices I ever made!

Jesus, lover of my soul. Thank You. I'm holding Your hand forever . . .

Lucinda Secrest McDowell
"Sunnyside," Wethersfield, CT
January 2019

About the Author

Lucinda Secrest McDowell, M.T.S., is passionate about embracing life—both through deep soul care as well as living courageously to touch a needy world. A storyteller who engages both heart and mind, she delights in *helping you choose a life of serenity and strength.*

A graduate of Gordon-Conwell Theological Seminary and Furman University, McDowell is the author of fourteen books and contributing author to more than thirty books. Her books include the award-winning *Dwelling Places*, as well as *Ordinary Graces, Live These Words,* and *Refresh!* She is a member of the Redbud Writers Guild and Advanced Writers and Speakers Association. Lucinda received Mt. Hermon Writer of the Year award and guest blogs for *The Write Conversation, Blue Ridge Mountains Christian Writers Conference,* and *(in)courage.*

Whether codirecting *reNEW—retreat for New England Writing and Speaking,* pouring into young mamas, serving on faculty for writing and speaking conferences, or leading a restorative day of prayer, she is energized by investing in people of all ages. Lucinda's favorites include tea parties, good books, laughing friends, ancient prayers, country music, cozy quilts, musical theatre, and especially her family scattered around the world doing amazing things. Known for her ability to convey deep truth in practical and winsome ways, she writes from her home, "Sunnyside" cottage, in New England and blogs weekly at EncouragingWords.net.

> Every word you give me is a miracle word—
> how could I help but obey?
> Break open your words, let the light shine out,
> let ordinary people see the meaning.
>
> —Psalm119:129–130 *The Message*

Mission: To glorify God and live in His grace and freedom, and through the power of the Holy Spirit to use my gifts to communicate God's faithfulness, extend His grace, and encourage others to trust Him fully.

Let's Stay Connected!
Website/Blog www.EncouragingWords.net
E-mail LucindaSMcDowell@gmail.com
Phone 860-402-9551
Twitter @LucindaSMcDowel
Instagram @LucindaSecrestMcDowell
Facebook Lucinda Secrest McDowell—Encouraging Words
Mail Encouraging Words, P.O. Box 290707, Wethersfield CT 06129 USA

Notes

1. Phillips Brooks, as quoted in *A Well-Tended Soul: Staying Beautiful for the Rest of Your Life* by Valerie Bell (Grand Rapids: Zondervan Publishing House, 2000), 44.

Day 1: Choose What Matters Most

1. Kathleen Norris, as quoted in *Liturgy of the Ordinary: Sacred Practices in Everyday Life* by Tish Harrison Warren (Downers Grove, IL: IVP Books, 2016), PDF e-book.

2. Emily P. Freeman, *The Next Right Thing: A Simple, Soulful Practice for Making Life Decisions* (Grand Rapids: Revell, 2019), 102.

Day 2: Choose Hope

1. Eugene H. Peterson, *A Long Obedience in the Same Direction: Discipleship in an Instant Society*, commemorative ed. (Downers Grove, IL: IVP Books, 2019), 70.

2. Victor E. Frankl, *Man's Search for Meaning: An Introduction to Logotherapy*, 4th ed. (Boston: Beacon Press, 1992), 75.

3. Peterson, *A Long Obedience in the Same Direction*, 140.

Day 4: Choose Silence

1. Adel Ahlberg Calhoun, *Spiritual Disciplines Handbook: Practices That Transform Us,* rev. and exp. (Downers Grove, IL: IVP Books, 2015), 123.

2. Ibid., 122–123.

Day 6: Choose Risk

1. Elisabeth Elliot, *The Savage My Kinsman* (Ann Arbor: Servant Books, 1981), 42.

2. Ibid., 29.

3. Melanie Shankle, *Church of the Small Things: The Million Little Pieces That Make Up Life* (Grand Rapids: Zondervan, 2017), 147.

Day 7: Choose to Listen

1. Shannan Martin, *The Ministry of Ordinary Places: Waking Up to God's Goodness Around You* (Nashville: Nelson Books, 2018), 27.

2. Henri J. M. Nouwen, *Bread for the Journey: A Daybook of Wisdom and Faith* (New York: HarperOne, 2011), PDF e-book, March 11.

Day 8: Choose Fearless

1. Max Lucado, *Fearless: Imagine Your Life Without Fear* (Nashville: Thomas Nelson, 2009), 13.

Day 10: Choose to Encourage

1. Mark Pattison, "Fred Rogers' ministry was on TV to kids, says documentarian," CatholicPhilly.com, June 4, 2018, http://catholicphilly.com/2018/06/culture/fred-rogers-ministry-was-on-tv-to-kids-says-documentarian/.

2. Tyler Huckabee, "11 Mr. Rogers Quotes Every Christian Should Read," *Relevant*, March 20, 2015, https://relevantmagazine.com/culture/10-mr-rogers-quotes-you-need-read.

3. Ibid.

Day 11: Choose Gratitude

1. Les Parrott, *You're Stronger Than You Think: The Power to Do What You Feel You Can't* (Carol Stream, IL: Tyndale House Publishers Inc., 2012), 134.

2. Ron Rolheiser, "The Major Imperatives within Mature Discipleship," Missionary Oblates of Mary Immaculate United States Province, April 15, 2018, https://www.omiusa.org/index.php/2018/04/15/the-major-imperatives-within-mature-discipleship-2/.

Day 12: Choose Obedience

1. Angie Smith, *For Such a Time as This: Stories of Women from the Bible, Retold for Girls* (Nashville: B&H Publishing Group, 2014), 114.

Day 13: Choose Blessing

1. John Ortberg, *Soul Keeping: Caring for the Most Important Part of You* (Grand Rapids: Zondervan, 2014), PDF e-book, chap. 13.

Day 14: Choose Connection

1. Alister McGrath, *If I Had Lunch with C. S. Lewis: Exploring the Ideas of C. S. Lewis on the Measuring of Life* (Carol Stream, IL: Tyndale House Publishers Inc., 2014), 46.

Day 16: Choose Release

1. "VOA Turkish Interview: Pastor Andrew Brunson," by Mehmet Toroglu, *VOA Turkish Service*, October 26, 2018, https://www.voanews.com/a/voa-turkish-interview-pastor-andrew-brunson/4631446.html.

2. Ibid.

Day 17: Choose Surrender

1. Oswald Chambers, *My Utmost for His Highest*, updated ed. (United States: Discovery House, 2010), PDF e-book, November 10.

2. A. W. Tozer, *The Pursuit of God*, as quoted in *The Tale of the Tardy Oxcart and 1,600 Other Stories* by Charles R. Swindoll (Nashville: Thomas Nelson Inc., 1998), PDF e-book.

Day 18: Choose Prayer

1. Janet Holm McHenry, *The Complete Guide to the Prayers of Jesus* (Minneapolis: Bethany House, 2018), 56.

2. Mark Batterson, *The Circle Maker: Praying Circles Around Your Biggest Dreams and Greatest Fears*, ex. ed. (Grand Rapids: Zondervan, 2016), PDF e-book, ch. 2.

3. Ibid., ch. 16.

Day 19: Choose Strength

1. Ashley Majeski, "'I'll Push You': Man pushes best friend in wheelchair 500 miles across Spain," *Today*, April 15, 2017, https://www.today.com/kindness/i-ll-push-you-man-pushes-wheelchair-bound-best-friend-t110422.

2. Emily McFarlan Miller, "'I'll Push You': Friends, one in a wheelchair, document their Spanish pilgrimage," *Crux*, November 2, 2017, https://cruxnow.com/global-church/2017/11/02/ill-push-friends-one-wheelchair-document-spanish-pilgrimage/.

3. Parrott, *You're Stronger Than You Think*, 131.

Day 20: Choose Love

1. Eugene H. Peterson, *Leap Over a Wall: Earthly Spirituality for Everyday Christians* (San Francisco: HarperSanFrancisco, 1997), 173.

2. Ibid.

3. Martin, *The Ministry of Ordinary Places*, 50–53.

4. Bob Goff, *Everybody, Always: Becoming Love in a World Full of Setbacks and Difficult People* (Nashville: Nelson Books, 2018), 218–219.

Day 21: Choose Patience

1. Tyler Edwards, "Christians Need to Recover the Lost Art of Patience," *Relevant*, July 26, 2016, https://relevantmagazine.com/life/christians-need-recover -lost-art-patience.

Day 22: Choose to Sing

1. Keith Getty and Kristyn Getty, *Sing! How Worship Transforms Your Life, Family, and Church* (Nashville: B&H Publishing Group, 2017), PDF e-book.

2. Mark Batterson, *Whisper: How to Hear the Voice of God* (New York: Multnomah, 2017), 16–17.

3. Hildegard of Bingen, "Historical Quotes," *Christianity Today*, accessed May 15, 2019, https://www.christianitytoday.com/history/quotes/.

Day 23: Choose With

1. Ortberg, *Soul Keeping*, PDF e-book.

2. Skye Jethani, *With: Reimagining the Way You Relate to God* (Nashville: Thomas Nelson, 2011), PDF e-book, ch. 6.

3. Harold Myra and Marshall Shelley, *The Leadership Secrets of Billy Graham* (Grand Rapids: Zondervan, 2010), PDF e-book.

Day 24: Choose Less

1. Courtney Carver, *Soul Simplicity: How Living with Less Can Lead to So Much More* (New York: TarcherPerigee, 2017), 94–95.

Day 27: Choose Covenant

1. Timothy Keller, *The Meaning of Marriage: Facing the Complexities of Commitment and the Wisdom of God,* with Kathy Keller (New York: Penguin Books, 2011), PDF e-book.

Day 28: Choose Joy

1. Peterson, *A Long Obedience in the Same Direction*, 95.

2. Henry Blackaby and Richard Blackaby, *Experiencing God Day by Day* (Nashville: B&H Publishing Group, 2006), 130.

3. Sally Clarkson, "Learning How to Choose Joy." www.sallyclarkson.com (blog), August 13, 2014, http://sallyclarkson.com/blog/learning-how-to-choose-joy.

Day 29: Choose Identity

1. John Eldredge, "The Sacred Romance: Drawing Closer to the Heart of God," in *Desire & Sacred Romance 2-in-1* (Nashville: Thomas Nelson, 2009), 88.

2. Jethani, *With*, PDF e-book.

3. Deidra Riggs, *Every Little Thing: Making a World of Difference Right Where You Are* (Grand Rapids: Baker Books, 2015), PDF e-book.

Day 30: Choose Forgiveness

1. Debbie Alsdorf and Joan Edward Kay, *It's Momplicated: Hope and Healing for Imperfect Daughters of Imperfect Mothers* (United States: Tyndale House Publishers Inc, 2018), 202.

2. Ibid., 203.

3. Ibid., 204.

4. Ibid., 210.

5. Blackaby and Blackaby, *Experiencing God Day By Day*, 49.

Day 31: Choose to Believe

1. A. W. Tozer, *The Knowledge of the Holy: The Attributes of God* (India: General Press, 2019), PDF e-book, ch. 1.

2. Stephen J. Binz, "Understanding five key purposes of the creed," *OSV News-weekly*, September 5, 2012, https://osvnews.com/2012/09/05/understanding-five-key-purposes-of-the-creed/.

Day 32: Choose Celebration

1. Brennan Manning, *The Ragamuffin Gospel* (Sisters, OR: 2000), 166.

Day 33: Choose Deep

1. Ken Shigematsu, *Survival Guide for the Soul: How to Flourish Spiritually in a World that Pressures Us to Achieve* (Grand Rapids: Zondervan, 2018), PDF e-book.

2. Mark Labberton, *Called: The Crisis and Promise of Following Jesus Today* (Downers Grove, IL: IVP Books, 2014), 45.

Day 35: Choose Stories

1. Peterson, *Leap Over a Wall*, 3–4.

Day 36: Choose to Dwell

1. Lucinda Secrest McDowell, *Dwelling Places: Words to Live in Every Season* (Nashville: Abingdon Press, 2016), ch. 23.

Day 37: Choose to Think

1. Tracie Miles, *Unsinkable Faith: God-Filled Strategies to Transform the Way You Think, Feel, and Live* (Colorado Springs: David C. Cook, 2017), PDF e-book, ch. 10.

2. Ibid., 103.

3. Ibid., 10.

Day 38: Choose Calm

1. Tricia Goyer, *Calming Angry Kids: Help and Hope for Parents in the Whirlwind* (Colorado Springs: David C. Cook, 2018), PDF e-book, intro.

2. Ibid., 135.

3. Douglas Noll, *De-Escalate: How to Calm an Angry Person in 90 Seconds or Less* (United States: Atria Books/Beyond Words, 2017), 10.

Day 39: Choose Grace

1. Victor Hugo, *Les Misérables*, trans. Isabel F. Hapgood (New York: Thomas Y. Cromwell Company Publishers, 1887), 101.

Day 40: Choose Power

1. Suzanne Burden, Carla Sunberg, and Jamie Wright, *Reclaiming Eve: The Identity and Calling of Women in the Kingdom of God* (United States: Foundry Publishing, 2014), 29.

2. Ibid., 29–30.

Day 41: Choose Self-Care

1. Lisa A. Beach, "6 Simple Self-Care Ideas for Busy Moms," Parents.com, accessed June 4, 2019, https://www.parents.com/parenting/moms/healthy-mom/6 -simple-self-care-ideas-for-busy-moms/.

2. April Yamasaki, "A Spirituality of Imperfection and Self-Care," *GodSpace* (blog), September 4, 2018, https://godspacelight.com/2018/09/04/a-spirituality-of -imperfection-and-self-care/.

Day 44: Choose Friendship

1. C. S. Lewis, in *The Quotable Lewis: An Encyclopedic Selection of Quotes from the Complete Works of C. S. Lewis*, eds. Wayne Martindale and Jerry Root (Wheaton, IL: Tyndale House Publishers, 2012), 238.

2. Catherin Hart Weber, "Pursuit of Happiness," in *A Faith and Culture Devotional: Daily Readings on Art, Science, and Life*, by Kelly Monroe Kullberg and Lael Arrington (Grand Rapids: Zondervan, 2009), 235–236

3. Peterson, *Leap Over a Wall*, 54.

Day 45: Choose Tears

1. Ingrid Trobisch, *Keeper of the Springs* (Sisters, OR: Multnomah Publishers, 1997), 67.

2. Jerry Sittser, *A Grace Disguised: How the Soul Grows through Loss* (Grand Rapids: Zondervan, 1995), 37 and 75.

Day 46: Choose True Beauty

1. Crystal Hodges, "My Photo Went Viral on Facebook for the Wrong Reason," The Mighty, May 21, 2015, https://themighty.com/2015/05/woman-responds -when-port-wine-stain-photo-goes-viral/.

2. Ibid.

3. Cindy K. Sproles, *Liar's Winter* (Grand Rapids, MI: Kregel Publications, 2017), 167.

4. Ibid., 168.

Day 47: Choose Battle

1. Eldredge, "The Sacred Romance: Drawing Closer to the Heart of God," 108.

Day 48: Choose Rescue

1. "Wesley to Wilberforce: John Wesley's last letter from his deathbed," Christian History, *Christianity Today*, accessed May 20, 2019, https:// www.christianitytoday.com/history/issues/issue-2/wesley-to-wilberforce .html.

Day 49: Choose Rest

1. John Ruskin, "Life Rests," in *Folded Hands*, ed. William B. Cairns (New York: American Tract Society, 1878), PDF e-book.

Day 50: Choose Nature

1. "About Lilias," Lilias Trotter, *Miriam Rockness: Reflections on the Art and Writings of Lilias Trotter*, accessed May 20, 2019, https://ililiastrotter.wordpress.com/about/.

2. Lilias Trotter, as quoted in *A Blossom in the Desert*, com. and ed. by Miriam Huffman (Rockness. Grand Rapids: Discovery House Publishers, 2007), n.p.

3. Bill Gaultiere, "Contemplating God in the Beauty of Nature," *Soul Shepherding* (blog), https://www.soulshepherding.org/contemplating-god-beauty-nature/.

4. John Edredge and Stasi Eldredge, *Captivating: Unveiling the Mystery of a Woman's Soul* (Nashville: Thomas Nelson, 2010), 35.

Day 51: Choose Humility

1. Michael M. Smith, *Becoming More Like Jesus* (Colorado Springs: NavPress, 1999), 54.

Day 52: Choose Compassion

1. Henri Nouwen, Donald McNeill, and Douglas Morrison, *Compassion: A Reflection on the Christian Life* (United States: Image, Doubleday, 2005), 3–4.

2. Sherrie Bourg Carter, "Are You Suffering from Compassion Fatigue?" *Psychology Today*, July 28, 2014, https://www.psychologytoday.com/us/blog/high-octane-women/201407/are-you-suffering-compassion-fatigue.

Day 53: Choose Life

1. Thornton Wilder, *My Town*, Acting ed. (United States: Coward-McCann Inc., 1965), 83.

2. C. S. Lewis, in "The Pursuit of Happiness: C. S. Lewis's Eudaimonistic Understanding of Ethics," by David Horner, in *In Pursuit of Truth: A Journal of Christian Scholarship*, April 21, 2009, http://www.cslewis.org/journal/the-pursuit-of-happiness-c-s-lewis's-eudaimonistic-understanding-of-ethics/.

3. Blaise Pascal, *Thoughts on Religion and Philosophy* (Glasgow: William Collins, 1838), 68.

Day 54: Choose Worship

1. Timothy Keller, *The Songs of Jesus: A Year of Daily Devotions in the Psalms* with Kathy Keller (New York: Viking, 2015), 142

Day 55: Choose Questions

1. Stephen Mattson, "13 Questions All Christians Eventually Ask Themselves," *Sojourners*, June 25, 2013, https://sojo.net/articles/13-questions-all -christians-eventually-ask-themselves.

2. Kellye Fabian, *Sacred Questions: A Transformative Journey through the Bible* (Colorado Springs: NavPress, 2018), viii.

Day 56: Choose Shelter

1. Anna Altman, "The Year of Hygge: The Danish Obsession with Getting Cozy," *The New Yorker*, December 18, 2016, https://www.newyorker.com/culture /culture-desk/the-year-of-hygge-the-danish-obsession-with-getting-cozy.

2. Trobisch, Keeper of the Springs, 20.

Day 58: Choose Legacy

1. Alsdorf, *It's Momplicated*, 224.

Day 59: Choose Discernment

1. Oswald Chambers, *My Utmost for His Highest*, classic ed. (United States: Discovery House, 2017), PDF e-book, August 13.

**If you enjoyed this book, will you consider sharing
the message with others?**

Let us know your thoughts at info@newhopepublishers.com. You can also
let the author know by visiting or sharing a photo of the cover on
our social media pages or leaving a review at a retailer's site.
All of it helps us get the message out!

Twitter.com/NewHopeBooks
Facebook.com/NewHopePublishers
Instagram.com/NewHopePublishers

———————

New Hope® Publishers is an imprint of Iron Stream Media,
which derives its name from Proverbs 27:17,
"As iron sharpens iron, so one person sharpens another."

This sharpening describes the process of discipleship, one to another.
With this in mind, Iron Stream Media provides a variety of solutions
for churches, missionaries, and nonprofits ranging from in-depth Bible
study curriculum and Christian book publishing to custom publishing and
consultative services. Through the popular Life Bible Study and Student
Life Bible Study brands, ISM provides web-based full-year and short-term
Bible study teaching plans as well as printed devotionals, Bibles,
and discipleship curriculum.

For more information on ISM and New Hope Publishers,
please visit

IronStreamMedia.com
NewHopePublishers.com

Also Available from Author
Lucinda Secrest McDowell

If you enjoyed this book, you'll love . . .

You are a prized possession. In this thirty-day devotional, hear the tender words of a loving Savior: you are My prize.

Available from NewHopePublishers.com and your favorite retailer.

A 30-Day Devotional

Prized

Experience the Tender Love of the Savior

Jennifer Kennedy Dean

author of Best-Selling *Live a Praying Life*

YOU MAY ALSO ENJOY . . .

BEAUTIFUL WARRIOR EMPOWERS YOU
TO BREAK FREE FROM THE INSECURITY
THAT HAS YOU TRAPPED.